HOW TO
cheat IN PHOTOSHOP
Elements 6

Create stunning photomontage images on a budget

David Asch and Steve Caplin

ELSEVIER

AMSTERDAM • BOSTON • HEIDELBERG • LONDON • NEW YORK • OXFORD
PARIS • SAN DIEGO • SAN FRANCISCO • SINGAPORE • SYDNEY • TOKYO
Focal Press is an imprint of Elsevier

Focal Press

Focal Press is an imprint of Elsevier
Linacre House, Jordan Hill, Oxford OX2 8DP, UK
30 Corporate Drive, Suite 400, Burlington, MA 01803, USA

First published 2008

British Library Cataloguing in Publication Data
A catalogue record for this book is available from the British Library

Library of Congress Cataloging-in-Publication Data
A catalog record for this book is available from the Library of Congress

ISBN: 978-0-240-52083-4

For information on all Focal Press publications visit our website at www.focalpress.com

Book design and cover by Steve Caplin

Printed and bound in Canada

08 09 10 11 11 10 9 8 7 6 5 4 3 2 1

Contents

Contents

How to cheat, and why

The truth about cheating

We've used the word 'cheating' in the title of this book in two ways. The most obvious is that we're describing how to make images look like photographs, when they're not. In this sense, it simply means creating photographic work without the need for a studio.

The other sense of 'cheating' is finding shortcuts to help you work more quickly and more economically. Wherever possible, we've used the quickest solutions we can find to achieve the results.

Each workthrough in this book is designed as a double page spread. That way, you can prop the book up behind your keyboard while going through the associated file on the CD.

At the end of each chapter you'll find an Interlude, in which we discuss an issue of relevance to the Elements artist. Some cover essential information about file sizes and types, color mode, and so on; others take a broader view. Think of them as light relief, and read them to save eye strain from staring at the screen for too long.

Who is the book for?

As the 'baby brother' to the full Photoshop CS3, Photoshop Elements has long suffered the stigma of being a cheap, unprofessional product. Cheap it may be: but it contains 90% of the features found in the full Photoshop and, as we've seen from user-created artwork, it's anything but unprofessional.

It's true that Elements is rarely used in a graphics studio or publishing company. But this is mainly because it doesn't include the high-end prepress features found in Photoshop: using Elements doesn't mean that you're working with a substandard application.

Some Elements users simply want to enhance their digital captures, perhaps adding a caption or two. But there are also those who want to take their work further: to explore the field of photomontage, and to make reality from the dreams locked in their heads. It's for these users that *How to Cheat in Photoshop Elements 6* will be of most benefit, helping them to release that potential and get their ideas out of their heads and onto the screen.

As a montage application, Elements is only as limited as your imagination. It can realize any montage you can conceive, as long as you have the technical skill required. We aim to provide you with that skill set, enabling you to unleash your creativity. Whether you're montaging missing family members into a group portrait, or creating a complex work of art, Elements can help you achieve your goal.

What's on the CD?

We've included all the photographic images from the workthroughs in this book on the CD, so that after reading about them you can open up the original files and experiment with them for yourself. There are also a number of QuickTime movies showing specific techniques in action: sometimes it's better to see how to achieve an effect than merely to be told about it.

The CD also includes a set of Layer Styles and custom Shapes that we've created in Photoshop. Although you can't create these effects in Elements, you can import them and apply them to your own artwork – and modify them to quite a large degree.

Going further

Visit the book's website at www.howtocheatinphotoshopelements.com and you'll find the user forum. This is where you can post questions or problems, and exchange ideas with other readers: we'll also do our best to solve any Elements-related issues that may be troubling you. If you get stuck, either on a tutorial in the book or elsewhere in Elements, this is your first place to look for a solution.

Steve Caplin and David Asch
London and Lewes, 2007

Acknowledgments

This book is dedicated to Jules and Carol, for putting up with us while we wrote it.

We're grateful to the following:

Asma Palmeiro and Emma Baxter of Focal Press, for their patience and persistence

Keith Martin, for helping create the keyboard shortcuts font

Adobe Systems Inc., for making Photoshop Elements

Many of the images in this book are from royalty-free photo libraries. Most of them are from the best subscription site we know, www.photos.com. With a huge range of royalty-free photographs available for download, it's always our first stop when we're looking for the perfect image. Many thanks to them for allowing us to include low resolution versions of many of their excellent pictures in the tutorials in this book.

How to use this book

We doubt if any readers of this book are going to start at the beginning and work their way diligently through to the end. In fact, you're probably only reading this section because your computer's just crashed and you can't follow any more of the workthroughs until it's booted up again. This is the kind of book you should be able to just dip into and extract the information you need.

But we'd like to make a couple of recommendations. The first four chapters deal with the basics of photomontage: making selections, working with layers, and adjusting your images. There are many Elements users who have never learnt how to make layer masks, or picked up the essential keyboard shortcuts. Because we talk about these techniques throughout the book, we need to bring everyone up to speed before we get to the harder stuff.

Although the book is designed for users of Elements 6, most of the tutorials will apply to those who have earlier versions of the program as well. We've indicated on each page where Elements 6 is specifically required to perform the task in hand.

The techniques in each chapter build up as you progress through the workthroughs. Frequently, we'll use a technique that's been discussed in more detail earlier in the same chapter, so it may be worth going through the pages in each chapter in order, even if you don't read every chapter in the book.

The CD icon on each tutorial page indicates that the source file for that tutorial is on the CD, so you can open it up and try it out for yourself. The Movie icon indicates that there's an associated QuickTime movie on the CD.

If you get stuck anywhere in the book, or in Elements generally, visit the Reader Forum, accessed through the main website:

www.howtocheatinphotoshopelements.com

This is where you can post queries and suggestions. We visit the forum every day, and will always respond directly to questions from readers. But expect other forum members to weigh in with their opinions as well!

■ The photograph of a woman in Ecuador, above, shows a strong face, brightly colored clothes and a neatly incongruous hat. But that background is just confusing: how much better it is when we change it for the view across the street. Removing the woman from her background is easier than you might think!

1

Selection techniques

WORKING IN PHOTOSHOP ELEMENTS almost always involves making selections. Whether you're combining images from several sources into a single montage, or simply replacing an overcast sky with a bright sunny one, you need to make selections within your image.

Elements offers a range of tools for the purpose. Some are automatic, and will find areas of similar color; some involve tracing around an object's edge; some combine the two methods, making complex selections easy to do.

Whether you're new to Elements, or an old hand, it's worth your while going through this chapter to make sure you're up to speed on the selection methods that are available to you.

Marquee selections

THE MARQUEE TOOL is the basic tool for making selections in Elements. Pressing **M** is the keyboard shortcut for this tool: pressing the key again will toggle between the standard rectangular Marquee, and the elliptical Marquee.

Every Elements user should be aware of the ability to hold the **Shift** key to draw a square or a circle, rather than a rectangle and an ellipse, and to hold **alt** to draw a selection from the center out.

We're not limited to just one selection at a time, however; by holding combinations of the **alt** and **Shift** keys, we're able to add and subtract additional selections – and we can even create intersections of the old and the new.

1 By default the Marquee Tool draws selections from corner to corner. Hold the tool as you drag, and when you release you'll have a rectangular selection, with the start and end points of the drag at opposite corners.

2 If you hold **alt** after you start to drag with the tool, it will draw a selection from the center out. This can be useful when you want, for instance, a circular selection centered on a point in the image.

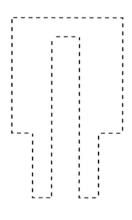

5 As well as adding to our existing selection, we can also subtract from it. This time, rather than the **Shift** key. hold down **alt** before starting to draw the new selection. This time, the thin vertical selection (above left) is

drawn on top of the existing selection. Note how now the crosshair cursor has a – sign next to it to show subtraction. Once this selection is removed from the original, we're left with the selection shown above right.

3 Holding **Shift** after you start to drag will turn a rectangle into a perfect square, and an ellipse into a perfect circle. This is essential for starting to draw square floor tiles, or even moons and suns.

4 Different things happen if you hold keys down *before* you begin to draw a selection. Here, the square is our initial selection; if we hold **Shift** before we make a new selection, the effect is to add the new selection

to the old one. Note how the cursor crosshair now displays a tiny + sign next to it to indicate an additional selection. The result of making the two selections, above left, is shown on the right.

The order in which you press the keys and the mouse button makes a difference to the result. Holding the keys shown here before pressing the mouse button will affect how the selections interact; pressing them afterwards will make a square or a circle, or draw from the center out.

One additional tip is to hold the Spacebar as you're drawing a selection. This will allow you to move the selection around while you're still drawing it: release the Spacebar (but not the mouse button) to continue.

6 The final key combination is a mixture of the two previous ones. If you hold **alt Shift** before making a new selection, the result will be the intersection of the new with the old: in other words, the area where the

two selections overlap. The cursor now shows a tiny x with the crosshair. The result of making an intersection of the original selection, above left, is shown in the selection above right.

7 All these key combinations work for elliptical as well as rectangular selections, and can be used in combination. To make this ring selection, above, we first painted a tiny dot to mark the center. An elliptical selection was made, holding **alt** to draw from the center out, and then adding **Shift** to make the ellipse into a circle. Next, we held **alt** before drawing to subtract from the selection, then released this key and, held **alt Shift** to draw another circle from the center out.

5

More selection tools

WE LOOKED AT the Marquee tools on the previous pages – but what if you want to make a selection that isn't rectangular or round? There are several other tools we can use for this purpose.

Here, we'll look at the Lasso, Magic Wand, and Selection Brush tools. While the Magic Wand selects a range of colors, the other two select only those regions you trace. They're three quite different tools, but they each have their uses, as we'll see here.

We're going to use all these tools to remove the sky from this photograph of the Statue of Liberty, beginning with the Magic Wand to select the bulk of the sky.

1 To select all the sky in this image, first use the Magic Wand tool (**W**). You can change the tolerance to select a smaller or wider range of colors: a setting of 32 works well. Click once to the left of Liberty's body, and you'll see a selection something like this.

2 The top right and bottom right corners weren't included in the selection, as the color there is just outside the range. To add to the selection, hold **Shift** and click with the Magic Wand in the top right corner. These colors are now added.

6 There's a problem with 'leakage' on the other shoulder as well, and we can use the Selection Brush to fix that. The book, however, has straight edges to it; even if we made the Selection Brush really tiny, we'd find it hard to trace those straight lines.

7 Instead, let's go back to the Lasso tool: this time, we'll use the Polygonal Lasso instead. Holding **alt** before we drag once more, click from inside the body onto each corner of the book to add that with a straight line selection.

3 We can see a few stray pixels – most probably dirt on the lens – above the book, and to the left. Rather than use the Magic Wand, switch to the Lasso tool (**L**). Hold **Shift** once more and draw a loop around the stray dots to add them to the selection.

4 We can add the sky between the crown and the shoulder with the Magic Wand, holding **Shift** as before. Now that we're zoomed in, we can see a problem: part of the pale green statue has inadvertently been selected along with the sky.

5 The best tool to use here is the Selection Brush (**A**). Since we want to subtract from the sky selection, hold **alt** as you drag over the area: everywhere within the radius of the tool will be removed from the selection.

8 Once we've done a little further tidying up, our statue is selected. Except, of course, that it's the sky that we've selected rather than Liberty herself. We need to inverse that selection, by pressing **ctrl Shift I**.

9 With Liberty now properly selected, we can make a new layer from her by pressing **ctrl J**. When we hide the original layer by clicking on the eye icon in the Layers palette, we see Liberty just cut out against a checkerboard background.

10 Once the original background has gone, we can replace it with anything we choose – such as this more appealing sky, for example. See the following chapter for more about working with layers.

The Magnetic Lasso tool

ALTHOUGH THE LASSO TOOL is useful for tracing outlines, it can be tricky to draw accurately with it. There is another method: the Magnetic Lasso is a variant. As its name implies, this tool sticks to the edges of shapes as you draw around them, making the process of cutting objects or people from their backgrounds very much simpler.

The tool isn't perfect, by any means; it's almost impossible for any computer program to figure out the difference between foreground and background objects with any degree of accuracy. But it's a real time saver, and can be used to make quick selections with ease.

To choose the tool, click on its icon in the Options bar when the Lasso tool is selected, or simply select it from the pop-up Lasso icon in the toolbar.

1 Start in one corner of the statue, and trace along the edge of the object, sticking as close as you can to it. We've zoomed in here and enhanced the Magnetic Lasso edge to show it more clearly. The tool places square 'anchor points' each time it marks a change in direction.

4 We'll hit a few more of these snags as we work our way around the figure; they occur each time Elements finds a strong line to follow. Once again, it's not a problem; simply delete the misplaced points, and then click the mouse button to add your own.

2 Right away, we hit a problem: when we get to the shoulder, the Magnetic Lasso wants to follow the gold bar, rather than the paler white cloth. No need to start again: simply press *Backspace* to remove the last placed points, backtracking along the traced line.

3 We can now force the tool to go in the direction we want. Drag a little way up the perimeter, and before Elements places another point, get in first by clicking the mouse button to place one of your own. Continue doing this until the tool recognizes the direction in which you're going.

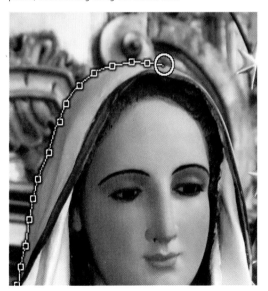

5 To make it easier to trace the outline, press the *Caps Lock* key on your keyboard. This will change the Magnetic Lasso icon to a circle, which shows the perimeter of the area in which it searches for boundaries.

6 When you get to the end of the object – in this case, the bottom right corner – it can be tricky to trace back along the bottom to the start, as the tool will think you're still looking for edges. Rather than get this wiggly line, press *Enter* to turn the path you've drawn into a selection.

HOT TIP

In step 5, we change the icon from a standard Magnetic Lasso to a circle showing the radius. You can make this larger and smaller using the Width setting on the Options bar; make it bigger for straightforward images, smaller for lots of fiddly edges.

The Edge Contrast and Frequency settings determine how much variation the tool looks for, and how often points are added to the path. In practice, you'll rarely need to change these from their default values.

9

Magic selection

WHILE IT WOULD BE POSSIBLE to select a complex image with just the Magic Wand and Lasso tools, there are easier ways to go about it.

On the previous pages, we looked briefly at the Selection Brush. This has a special variant, called the Magic Selection Brush, which appears on the Options bar when you choose the Selection Brush.

Like the Magic Wand, this tool selects areas of a similar color; the difference is that you begin by dragging the brush over a whole range of colors, and Elements does its best to figure out what you want to keep and what you don't want included in the selection.

This is seriously clever stuff. It doesn't always get it exactly right first time, of course, but it's flexible enough for you to make complicated selections in a very short time.

1 Begin by drawing a wiggly line with the Magic Selection Brush, over the person or object you want to cut out. The brush stroke will be shown as a red line. You don't have to be accurate here, but make sure you touch every different color within the object you want to select.

4 Again, Elements will make its selection once you release the mouse button. Now, we can see a huge difference: the person is largely correctly selected. There are a few holes (beneath her chin, the white area within the folds of material at her back) and her hat isn't properly selected, but we can fix that easily.

2 As soon as you release the mouse button, Elements will go to work and start turning that brush stroke into a selection. As we can see, a lot of the background has been included here – most of the wall, and large areas of the window. We can fix that next.

3 Hold *alt* before drawing with the brush again, and this will tell Elements which areas you don't want included in the selection. Now, draw a line over the background, being sure to paint over all the colors that aren't part of the person we want to cut out.

5 We can add the missing regions by painting with the Magic Selection Brush again if we wish. But since her hat's the same color as the window glass, it's always going to be tricky to select one and not the other. Far easier, in these circumstances, to switch to the regular Selection Brush.

6 It takes a small amount of experience to know when to persevere with the Magic Selection Brush, and when to just paint in the new selection with the regular Selection Brush. Paint to add to the selection; hold *alt* to subtract areas from it.

Magic extraction

1 Use the Foreground Brush (**B**) to drag within the area you want to keep. Make sure the brush touches areas like the hair, which could be mistaken for background.

SOME TYPES OF IMAGE are just too complex to cut out with the Magic Selection tool, or the Magic Wand; photographs such as this accordionist, with his complex instrument photographed against a busy background, would be tricky to trace with the Lasso or Selection Brush.

The Magic Extractor, however, offers a relatively quick and painless solution to this problem. It works within its own dialog, using a range of tools that combine to make difficult object selection far easier.

The precise order in which you use the tools depends on the image you want to cut out: but you always start with the Foreground and Background brushes, before moving on to fine tuning. Begin by choosing Magic Extractor from the Image menu.

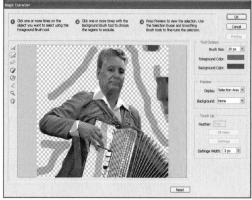

4 Use the Foreground Brush once more to drag a line over the keyboard, and the Background Brush to drag over those extra background elements.

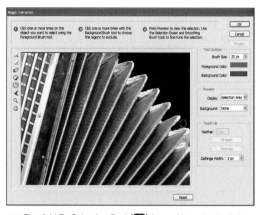

7 The Add To Selection Tool (**A**) is used to paint back in missing parts. Use a very small brush for fiddly areas, such as the edge of the accordion's bellows.

2 Switch to the Background Brush (**P**) and drag in areas you want removed. This brush paints a blue stroke, in contrast with the red of the Foreground Brush.

3 Now hit the Preview button to see how the extraction looks so far. There are some problems – pieces of stray background, and the keyboard's missing – which we can fix.

5 When we press Preview again, we can see a much better result. This is also a good time to change the preview background from None to Black, so we can see it clearly.

6 One or two stray background elements remain. We can remove these with the Remove From Selection Tool (**D**), which works like an eraser.

8 The extraction process does leave some ragged edges. Trace over the edge with the Smoothing Brush (**J**) to soften out the jaggies; hit OK when you're done.

Quick selection + refine edge

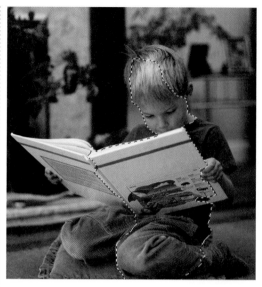

1 Begin by switching to the Quick Selection tool (**A**) and drag a single stroke from the center of the boy's head, across the book and down to his knee. We can see how the selection process guesses our intent: it's selected his face, most of the cover of his book, but stopped short at the pillow he's kneeling on.

NEW TO ELEMENTS 6 is the Quick Selection tool, which may well be the fastest method yet for cutting a person or object away from the background.

We've seen several selection methods already in this chapter, but they all involve a fair amount of work on the part of the user. The Quick Selection tool can help the process of lifting a complex subject from a complex background, quickly and painlessly.

The companion to this tool is the Refine Edge dialog, which processes the image after a selection has been made. Here, we can adjust the selection for an even better fit.

The image we'll work with here is of a boy reading in his living room. It's a tricky selection to make: both him and his surroundings include a range of colors and tones, making it harder for automatic selection to take place. But even in cases like this, we can perform the function with ease.

4 With our initial selection made, we can fine tune it by pressing the Refine Edge button on the Options bar above the image. This brings up the Refine Edge dialog: here we can smooth the selection, feather it (adding soft edges), and contract or expand it. This latter control is useful in cases where some background has inadvertently crept in.

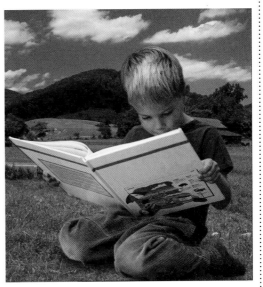

2 Let's add in the missing areas by dragging the tool over them. We don't have to do this all in one go: by default, any new strokes with this tool will add to the existing selection. As we can see here, we've now captured all but his right shoulder, his elbow and his sock; but we've also included a small piece of background below the book.

3 Reduce the size of the brush, and drag over the missing parts to include them in the selection. We can now remove the unwanted portions as well, by holding *alt* as we drag over them: as with all selections, holding this key removes the new selection from the original. WIth a little work, we can create a perfect selection.

5 While we're working with the Refine Edge dialog open, we can choose to view our image either with standard 'marching ants' selection borders, or with a red overlay. The second method gives us a much better idea of how our image will look as a cutout. We can now see precisely what's included, and what isn't.

6 Once the selection is complete, we can either delete the background or make a new layer from the selection. Adding a little smoothing can give unnaturally soft edges when seen against a plain white background, but by the time we've added a new background – such as this pastoral scene – the montage works well.

15

Working with selections

S O FAR IN THIS CHAPTER we've looked at how to make selections, using a variety of methods. Here, we'll look at what we can do with those selections when we've made them.

Selections can be filled in a variety of ways, both using dialogs and by pressing different key combinations. Selections can also be modified to make them soft-edged, and to make them larger and smaller.

1 We'll work mainly with circular selections here, for clarity – although any selection will work. To fill a selection with the current foreground color, press `alt` `←`; to fill it with the current background color, press `ctrl` `←`. (That's the Backspace key, rather than the left cursor arrow.)

2 If you hold `Shift` with either of these keys, it will fill with color but preserve the transparency of the current layer – as we can see here with this palmistry hand, which is on a layer of its own.

6 Once a selection has been made, we can press `ctrl` `alt` `D` to open the Feather dialog. Feathering softens the edges of the selection: the highger the radius, the softer the edge will be. After feathering the selection, we've here filled it with our foreground color.

7 We can 'load up' the area taken up by a layer by holding `ctrl` and clicking on the layer's thumbnail in the Layers palette. We'll use this process many times in this book.

3 Pressing *Shift* ⬅ will open the Fill dialog. There are several options: here, we're filling the circle with a pattern, as chosen from the 'Use' pop-up menu. Press OK to complete the fill process.

4 One of the more useful blending modes, as shown at the bottom of the dialog, is Behind. This fills the selected area behind the pixels already present on the current layer: the hand here remains fully visible.

5 We can also vary the opacity, or the strength of the fill. Here, we're filling with the current foreground color, but we're choosing to fill with an opacity of just 50%, so we can still see the hand through the filled circle.

8 We can move the selection itself with the cursor keys or by dragging it. Make sure a selection tool, rather than the Move tool, is active when you do this.

9 Here, we've feathered the selection (see step 6), and used Fill Behind (see step 4) to make a black shadow behind the key. The shadow is on the same layer as the key.

10 When we now duplicate the key layer a couple of times, and move and rotate it, the shadow travels with it; so each shadow is seen on the key below.

17

Setting up Elements

WHEN YOU BUY MOST APPLICATIONS, you can just install them and run them straight out of the box. (Or out of the zip archive in which you downloaded them, if you prefer.) And so, to some extent, you can with Elements; but there are a few tricks you can do to make the experience more comfortable.

It isn't that Elements is a particularly awkward program, but that since it involves working with images, it's memory hungry. It will happily gobble up all the RAM (memory) you allocate to it, and then sit panting for more. If it can't find any more real memory, it will settle for memory: using vast chunks of your hard disk to store temporary files while you're working. These 'scratch' files, as they're called, are slotted in around the other files on your hard disk, and are then deleted when you quit Elements. The more fragmented your hard disk, the more pieces these files will end up in, and the slower Elements will run. In the Interlude following Chapter 2, we'll look at the best way of coping with scratch files.

The Elements interface can be customized in a number of ways. Normally, you probably wouldn't bother to mess around with the interface of your applications – after all, the people who designed the program probably know it better than you do, so why not just trust their judgment and leave things as they are? Well, believe it or not, the people who designed Elements don't seem to spend that much time actually working in it. If they did, they wouldn't have the Project Bin turned on by default. Sure, it gives you access to all your currently open files: but it uses up an inch or more of valuable real estate. And that's an inch you could be using to view your pictures that much larger. Turn it off: you don't need to have it permanently on view. You can always pop it open when you need it.

The Palette Bin, down the right-hand side of the screen, contains your most frequently used palettes. Store your favorites here, but collapse them to just their title bars when you're not using them: they take up a lot of space, and you want to give the maximum amount of space to the Layers palette. When you have a document with a lot of layers in it, consider reducing the size of the thumbnails (using the pop-up menu at the top of the palette) to fit more in.

Auto Select Layer to activate a layer when you click it

Show highlight on rollover: helps to identify layers

Keep your most often used palettes available, but closed

Open palettes when you need them

Give as much space as you can to your Layers palette

Hide the Palette Bin to see more of your photographs

The Project Bin takes up valuable space: hide it away

When the Move tool is active, the Options bar will display a number of choices. Checking Auto Select Layer will mean that a layer is activated when you click on it, but this can happen by accident; when this is unchecked, you need to hold the Ctrl key when clicking on a layer to select it. You can also check the Show Highlight on Rollover box, which will pop up a blue rectangle surrounding each layer as you roll over it. This can help to identify layers, but can quickly become irritating. If you don't find the feature useful, turn it off. Similarly, the Show Bounding Box option will place handles around each selected layer. Again, this prevents you from seeing the image clearly; don't use it unless you find it helpful.

There's an option in the Preferences dialog to require the Shift key to be held when switching between tool variants – the Lasso, Magnetic Lasso and Polygonal Lasso, for instance. Checking this will mean you don't accidentally switch tools without meaning to.

This little chap seems overwhelmed by all the gifts. If they had all been placed directly onto the photo, it woud be stuck like that. Using layers in our image means we can freely move them around. Now we can clearly see that, like most children, he's not really interested in the gifts at all; he's perfectly happy playing with one of his balloons.

Montage essentials: layers

WHEN CREATING A MONTAGE, layers are probably the most important part of the process. Aside from the design itself, of course. Without them, creating complex composite images would be a slow and difficult process. Think of layers as individual celluloid sheets: each one can be laid on top of (or beneath) another to build up the artwork. These can be manipulated independently without affecting the rest of the picture. There are many different types of layer, too, as we'll see.

In this chapter we'll be using techniques that demonstrate the many functions and abilities of the main layer types. Beginning with the basics and on through to more advanced concepts, we'll see how layers are created, controlled and can be made to interact with each other in a variety of different ways.

Three card tricks

1 We've begun by creating a new document *ctrl* **N**. There are numerous presets to choose from or you can, as shown here, create one to your own specific dimensions. The background content defaults to white. We'll leave it as it is. We can always change its color later.

W HEN YOU CREATE A NEW DOCUMENT, it consists of a single layer: the background. This is your blank canvas. You can paint on it, run most filters and perform many other operations. But working on a single layer is very limiting, and you'll probably find yourself continuously reaching for the undo command. Although a painter will create his art directly on the canvas, we don't have to. Using layers allows us to add, remove and arrange pieces of our artwork; making as many changes along the way as we need.

The following example demonstrates the fundamentals of building a simple montage of playing cards using layers. We'll see how layout of the artwork can be changed simply by altering the order in which the layers appear and by either adjusting their visibility or hiding them completely.

4 The order of the layers is not fixed, of course. Click and hold the queen layer's thumbnail in the layers palette. Now drag it up above the king's layer. An indicator line will appear over its thumbnail. Release the mouse. The queen is now sitting on top of the other two cards.

7 Layers can also be turned on and off. Click the eyeball next to the layer you wish to hide. If you hold *alt* and click, it will hide all the other layers (including the background). This is particularly useful when you need to remove the clutter temporarily.

2 The first card has been added on its own layer. This can be done in several ways: the most common is by dragging the image from another document using the Move tool. In the latest versions, a file can be imported directly into the document using the File > Place command.

3 Here is the artwork with all three cards. As each is added, its layer is placed above the previous one. This gives the impression of the cards overlapping each other. The layer palette shows the structure; the top layer (the king) being the foremost card in the image.

Although it's easy to see which layers are which in a simple montage such as this, it's always good practice to give your layers meaningful names as they are added: Finding *Jack of Hearts* will be far easier than *Layer XX* when working on a complex piece of artwork with dozens of layers. Simply double-click the layer's label and replace it with your own.

5 You can, of course, add blank layers. We've made the background layer active by clicking its thumbnail. A new layer is added by clicking the new layer icon at the top of the layer palette. In this example it's been filled with color and some Gaussian noise to represent the fabric of a card table.

6 The transparency of a layer can be adjusted. This is achieved with the opacity slider in the layers palette. This ranges from invisible (0%) to completely solid (100%). The queen's opacity has been lowered to 50%. The rest of the image can now be seen through it.

8 For a more permanent solution, you can delete unwanted layers. This is done either by selecting the layer and clicking the trash icon or by clicking and dragging the layer's thumbnail onto it. Here we've made all the layers visible again and disposed of the queen.

9 Here's our final image displayed as it would look if you could view its component layers in three dimensions. Although the background layer appears as the same size as the other layers in the palette, it is represented here as an infinite base on which the rest of the images sit.

23

Divide and multiply

O N THE PREVIOUS PAGE, we created a
piece of artwork by importing individual
images as layers. The composition was altered
simply by reordering the structure and changing
their visibility. In the following tutorial we'll
go a stage further. Using the Move tool and
a combination of keyboard shortcuts we'll
reposition and duplicate a single layer to quickly
create multiple copies of the same object.

In the most recent versions of Elements,
multiple layers can be selected to form a
temporary group allowing us to manipulate
them as a single item. This is a much better way
of working as there is no need to merge the
layers into one before duplicating them, as was
the case with earlier revisions of the program.

1 Here's our single plate. Its shadow has been created
using a layer style; we'll be covering these later in the
chapter. Notice how the shadow from the shelf falls across
the plate. This is because both the shelves and their shadows
are on a separate layer in front of the rest.

4 Go to the Layers palette. Hold *Shift* and click the first
plate layer. This will highlight all three layers and in
doing so, temporarily group them together. Use the same
keyboard shortcut as before; this time, drag the cursor
straight down to create a copy of the entire row.

2 Make sure the plate layer is active by clicking its thumbnail in the Layers palette. Select the Move tool **V**. Click and hold the cursor over the plate. Now drag it across to the left edge of the shelf. Additionally, you can hold **Shift** to constrain the movement.

3 Hold the **alt** and **Shift** keys. Now click and drag the plate over to the right. Instead of simply moving it, this action has created a copy of the plate on a new layer. Release the mouse but keep the keys held. Now click on the new plate and drag once more to create the third.

HOT TIP

Make sure the Move Tool's Auto Select Layer option is disabled in the Options Bar. Whilst this feature can be useful for finding a layer buried deep in your artwork, it can also cause chaos. You may find yourself moving or copying the wrong part of your image if you accidentally click another layer instead of your intended target. You can mimic this function at any time by holding **ctrl** and clicking the layer in the document.

5 Leave the previous grouping enabled. Create a duplicate set for the final row. If you need to retain the group on a more permanent basis, click the chain icon at the top of the Layers Palette. An icon will appear to the right of each layer denoting that it is part of a linked set.

6 Currently there are nine separate plate layers. If you don't intend to make changes on an individual basis, you can flatten them into three rows or even one single layer. To do this, use the multiple select feature to group the layers together. Finally, press **ctrl E** to merge them.

Staying in shape

S O FAR, WE'VE LOOKED AT RASTER LAYERS.
These are the most common types but
do have one major downfall: resizing causes
permanent image quality loss. There is, of
course, no compromise when working with
photographs but if you use a lot of graphic
objects in your artwork, shape layers are the
perfect solution. Instead of being built up
from individual static pixels, vector shapes
are defined by anchor points; when scaled up
or down, the computer redraws the lines and
curves between the points – a digital 'join the
dots' image. No matter how many times the
graphic is scaled, there is never any degradation.

In the following example we'll use some of
the basic shape tools to create a film negative.
This could be used as a custom frame for your
photos or as a banner or header on a web
page. We'll see how areas can be added and
subtracted to alter the shape in a similar way
to the selection techniques covered in the first
chapter. You can, of course, perform all the
same functions as regular layers, too.

1 Select the Rectangular shape tool **U**. Choose a suitable
color from palette in the options toolbar; the dark red
orange preset works well. Click and drag out the base shape
for the frame. Deceptively, individual negative frames are
almost square; being only a little wider than they are tall.

4 Repeat the last step six times to finish the row; you
should have 8 holes. Grab the Shape Selection tool.
Click one of the hole shapes. Holding **Shift**, click each of the
other shapes to select them all. Hold **alt** **Shift**. Click and
drag down to duplicate the row on the bottom.

2 Press and hold **alt**. The cursor will show a minus sign next to the crosshair indicating subtract mode. This will remove the marked area. Draw another rectangle. This time make it wider: photo-shaped, as it were. Press the Spacebar whilst dragging to position the frame centrally.

3 Select the Rounded Rectangular shape tool. Hold **alt** again. Draw a small rectangle. Now hold **ctrl alt**. Click and drag the new shape to create a copy. Hold **Shift** to constrain the movement. Make the distance between them slightly larger than the size of the hole.

5 At present all the shapes are separate entities. It's unlikely we'll need to alter them. Click and drag a bounding box around the entire object. Now click the Combine button in the options toolbar. This creates a single shape from its component parts.

6 We've used the Custom Shape tool to add a direction arrow. This is created on a separate layer which, along with the text is grouped and linked to the film strip. Whilst it may not be the most tidy of solutions, you still benefit from the ability to scale the artwork image without loss of quality.

HOT TIP

Once you've completed your artwork, save it as a Photoshop document. This way you can be sure the layer information is retained correctly. You can then open and import the layer(s) into your artwork as and when you need it. Once you have it in place, you can alter the blend mode and opacity to suit. The frames can also be tiled seamlessly to create a strip.

Adding a little style

1 Styles can be added by double-clicking their thumbnail, highlighting and clicking the Apply button at the base of the Artwork and Effects palette or by dragging and dropping onto the target layer. In the example, we've applied the low drop shadow preset.

LAYER STYLES ARE VERSATILE, REUSABLE effects. With them you can quickly place shadows under objects, create metal textures, add embossing and much more. Unlike filters, however, they are non-destructive; once applied, they can be altered, added to or removed without the need to undo previous changes or recreate parts of the artwork. Styles are not limited to regular image layers either; in fact, they show their worth far better when applied to objects which themselves are changeable such as shape or text layers.

With version 6 of the program comes a much better settings dialog with which to fine tune the styles. Previous editions still gave you control over the attributes but these were fairly rudimentary in comparison. You will, of course, still be able to follow the majority of this tutorial.

4 We'll adjust the shadow next. Start by lowering the size. This makes it sharper, as though the light source were closer to the text. Increasing the distance value gives the appearance of the text being further from the background. You can also lower the opacity if required.

7 Because the style affects the layer as a whole, you have the ability to change the content of the layer without the need to apply the style again. In the example, the color and wording of the text has been changed; the style is aeded as we type. This even works when painting on a layer.

2 The default settings of the styles may not always be right for the image you are working on. Double-click the star (*f* on earlier versions) icon to the right of the layer thumbnail to open the settings dialog. Here you'll see the adjustments that can be made to the style's attributes.

3 We'll start by making the bevel a little smaller to fit the text better. Use the slider to lower the value; you'll see the effect change as you do so. Bring it down enough to make the bevel's ridges straight with a slight flatness on top. Here a value of around 12 pixels is sufficient.

HOT TIP

Although styles are normally cumulative, you can force the current effect to be replaced outright by holding *Shift* when applying the new style. Be aware that many of the more complex built-in presets will override your effects as they already contain compound settings. It's also worth noting that patterned styles on surfaces in perspective may not look right; particularly those which contain strong horizontal or vertical lines. Such effects are generally designed to be applied to flat objects. You'll need to simplify (flatten) the style, then create the distortion on the object.

5 The Lighting Angle controls the highlight and shadow of the bevel effects as well as the direction of the drop shadow. The default is top-left. This can be changed within the dialog. You can also click and drag within the document itself. This allows you to set the angle visually.

6 Styles can also be copied to new layers. Press and hold *alt*. Click and drag the original layer's style icon onto the new layer's thumbnail. The text adopts the exact same effect. This is useful when you have customized the style and to match it across the artwork.

8 The effects also operate independently to the layer. Here both layers have been flipped vertically. You'd expect the bevels and shadows to follow suit. Instead, they retain their original direction. One more thing to note: altering the lighting angle will affect all layers with a style applied.

9 Now you've set up your styles, what if you want to remove them? You can hide/show all styles from the Layer Styles sub-menu under the main Layer menu. You can also clear them from there (the same as deleting). This is also available from the More fly-out in the Layers Palette.

29

The power of adjustment

WHEN YOU APPLY AN ADJUSTMENT such as Levels to an image, the affected pixels are permanently altered. If at a later stage decide you no longer want that effect, unless you made a backup, you have a problem. It would, of course, be really helpful if you could create the same effect but have the ability to turn it on and off, alter its settings and have it apply to only certain areas of the image and, most importantly, be able to return to the image at any stage to do so. With Adjustment layers you can do just that. Anything beneath them in the layer stack will be affected unless, of course, you don't want it to. They are just like regular layers. You can alter their opacity, change the blend mode. Most importantly, however, they can be toggled on and off, disabling the effect.

In the following tutorial we'll use a Hue/Saturation adjustment layer to remove the color from a selected part of our image. This is done using the layer's built in mask. We'll see how it can be edited, inverted and even exchanged for a completely different effect.

1 Our image comprises two layers, the garden background and the man watering the plant. Hold *ctrl* and click the gardener's layer thumbnail to load its selection. Now press *ctrl* *Shift* *I* to inverse it. When we create our adjustment layer it will only affect the background.

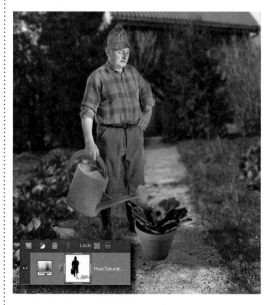

4 You might decide that you want the flowerpot in gray, too. Click the mask thumbnail to make it active. Grab the brush tool. Set the foreground color to white. Now carefully paint over the pot to remove its color. You're really just reducing the mask's protection over the layers.

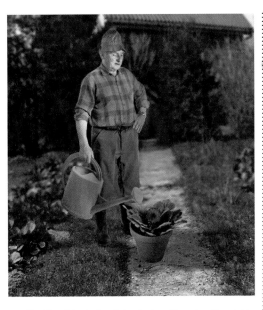

2 Create a Hue/Saturation adjustment layer from the split circle icon at the top of the Layers palette. Notice how the selection has been used to isolate the man in the layer mask. The black areas will not be affected by the changes we are going to make with the adjustment layer.

3 Use the slider in the dialog to drop the saturation right down. The background will become black and white, the man remains untouched. Notice how some color is still showing through the shadow. The gray tones act like an opacity filter. This will be explained later in the book.

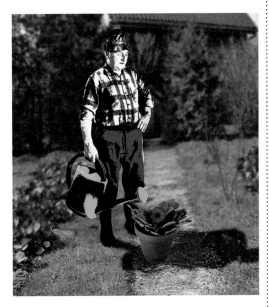

5 We can also swap the effect around, giving the background color back and removing it from the man. Press *ctrl* *I*. This inverts the layer mask; everything that was white is now black and vice versa. This acts like a toggle. Inverting again will revert it to its previous state.

6 Another feature is the ability to change the type of adjustment layer to use without losing the mask and any changes you might have made. Select Change Layer Content from the Layer menu. You can choose one of the 10 remaining to apply to the image; Posterize in the example.

HOT TIP

You can use adjustment layers to make temporary alterations to an image. For example, you may be having difficulty selecting and separating your subject from its background because there are areas of low contrast or it's simply too dark in places. Create a Brightness/ Contrast adjustment layer above it. You can take the values to their extremes for the duration of the task. Afterwards, you can simply turn the layer off or discard it completely.

Exploring blend modes

EVEN IF YOU'VE NEVER USED THEM you will no doubt be familiar with the term Blend Modes. These determine how layers interact with the other layers in the artwork. In our example, we'll change the grafitti layer's mode which will affect the way it blends with the wall; our background layer. There isn't space to show every mode but the examples should serve as a guide; the results you get will vary greatly depending on the the colors and tones of the component layers in your image.

1 The default is Normal. Technically this isn't really a blend mode at all as the top layer does not interact with the base layer; apart from its transparency. Almost all layer types can use blend modes. Individual tools such as the paint brush and gradients use them as well.

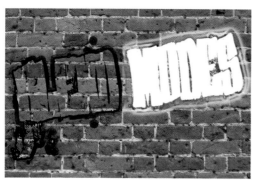

4 Here we have Multiply on the left and Screen on the right. Multiply produces rich darker tones. Again, white has no effect and is cancelled out. The opposite, Screen produces a much brighter blend. White is completely opaque. Any black in the image has no effect and is not displayed.

5 Color Burn (left) and Color Dodge (right) produce similar results to Multiply and Screen. The colors, however, appear far more exaggerated using these modes. Following on from these are Linear Burn and Linear Dodge (not shown). These produce slightly stronger results.

8 Hard Light, Vivid Light (shown here on the left) and Linear Light all produce strong color tones, Linear being the deepest. Pin Light (right) uses the tones of the base image to shift the color of the top layer, depending on lightness. 50% gray is invisible in all of these modes.

9 Hard Mix limits the blending image to eight colors – white, black, red, green, blue, yellow, cyan, and magenta the mix depends on the blending colors of both layers. This produces a result similar to that of posterize. It is a brash, aliased effect and therefore has limited use.

2 This is Dissolve. On a crisp, fully opaque image this mode has no effect. However, when you add some blur or start to lower the opacity, random pixels will start to disappear. The more the image is blurred, the stronger the effect becomes. You can see this on the sprayed green edge.

3 On the left we have Darken. This blends any pixels that are lighter than the wall: white becomes transparent. There's little change in the color. On the right is its counterpart, Lighten. This has the opposite effect, blending where the wall is darker. The color is a little washed out.

HOT TIP

Because using blend modes can produce very different results depending on the number of blended layers, their tonal values and many other factors, it's often easier to cycle through the individual modes until you find one that fits the effect you're looking for. There's a keyboard shortcut for this: press *Shift* + to drill down the list and *Shift* − to drill up. Make sure you're not in one of the painting modes as that will result in changing the mode for that tool, rather than the layer.

6 This is Overlay. It's a combination of Multiply and Screen. It darkens lighter pixels and vice versa. In areas of midtones there is little or no effect; 50% gray being completely invisible. The highlight and shadows are retained giving it a slightly blown out appearance.

7 Soft Light operates in a similar way to Overlay. The difference being it combines Darken and Lighten. As you can see, this produces a somewhat muted blend. This mode is often used for creating reflections because of its already slightly translucent qualities.

10 In Difference mode color is subtracted from either the base layer or the blend layer, depending on brightness. Pure white inverts the blending colors, black has no effect. This can be used for comparing images for slight changes. Exclusion (not shown) gives a less contrasted effect.

11 The four remaining modes: Hue, Saturation, Color and Luminosity work by combining the named attribute of the top layer with the remaining two (Color is not included) from the base. The example is Luminosity which discards the grafitti's color information, leaving only its brightness values.

Banqueting arrangements

A FEATURE INTRODUCED in Elements 5 was the ability to automatically align and distribute layers within the document. In earlier versions, this would have needed to be done by hand; either by sight alone or by setting up and aligning to a grid – a somewhat messy business. Now you can accurately space out and arrange components evenly across your artwork with just a few clicks of the mouse. This is great for making precise designs such as navigation bars on web pages or for laying out and ordering text and images for scrapbook pages.

1 Here we have the all the pieces of our place setting on separate layers. We could, of course, select and position each individual layer manually; but this is time consuming and not altogether accurate. Instead, let's make use of

Elements' ability to select and work with multiple layers simultaneously. By grouping the sets of cutlery together we can then use the new Align/ Distribute feature of the Move tool to space them out neatly either side of the plate.

3 Now we can space the cutlery out. The Distribute function works by spacing the central layer(s) evenly between the two outer ones. Start by arranging the knives and forks into two rough groups. The forks have already been

tidied in the example. Multi-select the inner and outer knives by again holding *ctrl* and clicking their name labels. Now use the Horizontal Centers option from the Distribution menu. They will now be evenly spaced.

2 The first task is to bring the plate into the center of the canvas. Select the Move tool **V**. Click the background layer in the Layers palette to make it active. Now hold **ctrl**. Click on the plate layer's name (not the thumbnail) to group the two layers. Start by selecting Horizontal Centers from the Align menu in the Options toolbar. This will shift the plate across to the middle. Now use the Vertical Centers option to move it down.

HOT TIP

You can also align layers to selections as well. We've used this method in the final step to match the cutlery to the baseline of the plate. If we had only used a layer group, everything would have been aligned to the base of the entire document.

4 Press **ctrl** and click the plate layer's thumbnail to load its selection. Now group all the cutlery layers together. You can do this by holding **ctrl** and dragging a bounding box across the document to encompass the knives. You'll see the layers highlighted in the palette. Release the mouse and do the same for the forks. Go back to the Align menu. This time select Bottom Edges. All the cutlery wil move down to align with the bottom of the plate.

Keep up, no slacking

THERE'S ONLY ONE THING FASTER than the speed of light: the computer industry. It seems that no sooner do you remove the shrink-wrap from your software or prize the new PC from its snug Styrofoam packaging; you expect to see a little fortune cookie style note congratulating you on your purchase being out of date. That groaning, creaking sound you hear becoming progressively louder is not your antiquated computer about to keel over in a spectacular shower of sparks, but the heavy cogs of the corporate machine trundling toward you, decimating all but the newest of technologies in its path.

As with the fashion industry, it seems you're nobody unless you're first in line for this season's must have accessory. As the glossy adverts in magazines will imply and the even glossier sales people in computer stores will tell you (the prospect of a sales commission instantly makes you an expert, of course), your current system is already half way to the scrap heap and not fit for anything other than being the basis for a retro art statement.

You should not be too despairing of the seemingly decrepit piece of hardware chugging away beneath your desk, or that your copy of Whizz-Bang 3000 Professional Gold Edition SP5 is now 'so last Tuesday'. Before you rush out to part with a month's salary, you have to ask yourself: *is it good enough for my purposes and, if it lacks a certain area of functionality, can I achieve the same thing in a different way?* Unless the latest hardware or software is offering something completely revolutionary, the answer will almost certainly be yes.

There will, of course, come the time where an upgrade is necessary. Perhaps support for your current operating system is being dropped and its replacement will not run efficiently on your computer. It may also be that certain components, such as graphics cards, need replacing. This doesn't involve replacing the whole system.

Ask anybody in the world of digital imaging – unless they're trying to sell you a completely new computer – what, above all, are the most important system components and you'll generally get the same answer: memory and hard disk space. Even if you have the latest AMTEL liquid-cooled, 50 megagiga-googleplex processor, it is still very much at the mercy of these two commodities. The computer needs memory to run the graphics program itself and store the image(s) you are currently working on, not to mention everything else that's going on in the background. Adobe recommends between 512Mb-1Gb for the current version of Elements to run smoothly. The more complex the document becomes, however, the more memory it needs to use to hold that information. Images can often bloat out to hundreds of megabytes in size, especially when you start creating multiple layers. Add to that the history (undo) states and the space used by copying and pasting to the clipboard and you'll soon be pushing the resources to their limits.

There's no way to second-guess how much memory you will need. Presently the average PC comes with around 1-2 Gigabytes, which is ample for most tasks. When the system starts running low on physical memory, it starts to free it up by using virtual memory, referred to as 'scratch' space in Elements. This is a temporary area on the hard disk set aside for storing the overflow. Think of it as writing things down on a scrap of paper when you begin to become overwhelmed with information. This is where you need to make sure you have a large enough hard disk. Remember, the operating system, programs and your data all share this space. If it's full to bursting, trying to cram in this transient file will at best slow things down to a crawl; at worst it can cause the program (or the entire system) to crash, taking whatever you are working on with it.

Enhancing your system needn't be expensive. A large external hard drive will set you back around $100-200; you just plug them in and they're ready to go with no fuss. An internal drive could be half that amount. You can add an extra gigabyte of memory for less than $50. If you're not technically minded and unwilling to delve into the arcane world that is the inside of your computer, there will usually be someone you know who can help. If not, there will be no shortage of people advertising in the classified section of the newspaper who will be able to do the work – usually for a reasonable price, too. If it keeps you up and running for a year or two more, it's certainly money well spent.

This photograph of a man rowing has been removed from its original background and placed into a tranquil river setting. It looks far more part of the scene when it's partially hidden behind the foliage: that, and the reflection in the water, really bring the scene to life.

3 Hiding and showing

CREATING EFFECTIVE PHOTOMONTAGES is all about making layers interact with each other. And more often than not, this entails making layers partially hidden behind existing objects in the scene.

The standard way to do this is to erase the parts you don't want. But this is an irrevocable step; instead, we'll look at a cheat that gives Elements users some of the power of Photoshop CS3, with the ability to selectively hide and show regions of layers.

We'll also see how to blend layers together in a convincing manner, and how to arrange our montages so that they look that bit more convincing.

Cheating with layer masks 1

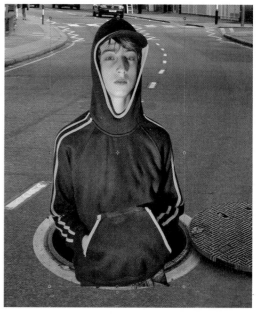

ONE OF THE MAJOR FEATURES present in the full version of Photoshop – but not found in Elements – is Layer Masks. These are a method of hiding, rather than deleting, parts of a layer in such a way that we can reveal them later if we need to.

It's a hugely powerful technique, as it means you never have to commit yourself to removing parts of a layer that you might want to get back. It's just a pity this technolocy isn't included in Elements as well.

Or isn't it? Well, in a way it is. We can use the fact that, in Elements, although layers themselves might not have masks, Adjustment layers still do. Which means that with a clever workaround, we can harness that power and put it to good use. Here, we'll use it to stick a boy down a drain.

1 Here's Steve's son Joe in front of the drain. The first thing we're going to do is to make a new Brightness & Contrast Adjustment layer, from the pop-up menu at the top of the Layers palette: use the default settings and press OK.

4 Now for the clever part. If we change the foreground color from black to white, we can paint the layer in again: now that we can see the edge of the hole, it's easy to paint it back in accurately, and the layer is revealed again.

40

As well as painting in black and white, you can paint on the Adjustment layer's mask in shades of gray: the darker the shade, the more the layer grouped with it will be hidden.

When painting on masks, you'll frequently want to switch between black and white. Press **X** to do this.

In step 6, you might find that some of Joe is visible at the bottom of the image. If so, just paint it out in black on the Adjustment layer mask.

2 We want to group Joe with the Adjustment layer, so switch to his layer and press **ctrl G**. Now click on the white rectangle to the right of the mask's icon in the Layers palette, because that's where we'll paint.

3 When we paint on this mask in black, we hide the Adjustment layer. Because Joe is grouped with it, we hide him as well. Using a hard-edged brush, paint out roughly around the edge of the drain and below it.

5 To give the effect of shading, switch to a large soft edged brush at an opacity of 50%, and paint in black at the front of the hole. This partially hides the layer, making Joe look shaded as he disappears into the drain.

6 Now for the *really* clever part. Because Joe's layer is separate from the Adjustment layer, we can move it independently. Here, we can drag Joe down and the mask stays in place, so it appears that he's going down the drain.

41

Cheating with layer masks 2

ON THE PREVIOUS PAGES we looked at how to fool Elements into thinking it could work with layer masks, by grouping a layer with an Adjustment layer beneath it.

It's a neat solution, and it makes it easy for anyone to use layer masks in Elements. But it's slightly clumsy having to manipulate two separate layers, when all you really want is to have a layer mask on one.

So here's another workaround. As we said earlier, Elements may not have layer masks built in, but Photoshop does. So what? Well, it turns out that Elements is capable of opening all Photoshop documents – including those with layer masks. And, surprise surprise, the layer masks come in to Elements intact, and we can use them as we wish.

On the CD you'll find a file called Layer masks PS.psd. It's an empty Photoshop layer with a mask attached: here's how to use it in your own artwork.

1 When you open Layer masks PS.psd you'll find it's a very small file. No matter: simply use the Image Size dialog to resize it to literally any size you want. Because both the layer and the mask are empty, there's no problem doing this.

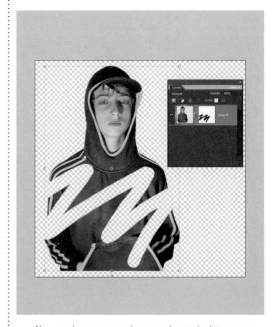

4 Now, we have a proper layer mask attached to our own layer, right in Elements. We can paint on it in black to hide the layer, and paint in white to reveal it again – or in shades of gray for partial transparency.

2 Now that we have our empty layer resized, let's see what we can do with it. Here, we've copied and pasted the picture of Joe from the previous tutorial: we've made the file big enough to hold him.

3 Position your layer above the layer that contains the mask, and press *ctrl* **E** to merge the layers together. In Elements 5 and earlier, you'll see a dialog asking what you want to do about the layer mask: press the Preserve button.

HOT TIP

Bringing layer masks into Elements unlocks a hidden feature that we weren't supposed to know about. The best thing is that you don't need to own the full version of Photoshop in order to make use of it: we've provided the Photoshop file for you, and you can use it in all your own projects.

If you ever want to see how a layer looks without its mask, hold *Shift* and click on the layer mask's thumbnail. This will temporarily disable it, placing a red X across the thumbnail. Use *Shift* click to enable the mask once more.

5 So let's put our new layer mask to work. Here, we've placed Joe onto a river background, and painted out around the bottom half of his torso to partially submerge him in the river.

6 Rather than painting on the mask, we can simply adjust it. Here, we can use the Brightness/Contrast adjustment to increase the brightness of the mask: this makes it less strong, so we can see his body beneath the water. Brilliant!

43

Smudge masking

S O FAR, WE'VE LOOKED AT CREATING
layer masks by painting on them with
the Brush tool. It works well: we can paint on
an adjustment layer's mask beneath our target
object to hide and show the object that's
grouped with it.

But we can use any of the painting tools, not
just the brush. Here, we'll look at how we can
use the Smudge tool to create a convincing
grass effect, using a technique that's far easier
than painting each blade.

1 First, create a new adjustment layer beneath the pot, as
described earlier in this chapter. Hold `ctrl` and click on
the pot's thumbnail to load it up, then inverse the selection
using `ctrl` `Shift` `I` ; fill the inverted area on the layer mask
with the foreground color (black) using `alt` `Backspace`.

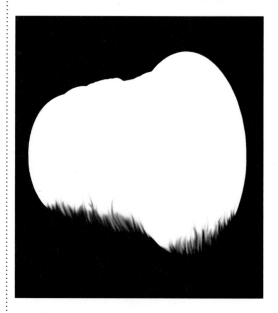

4 Here's how the finished adjustment layer's mask looks
on its own. Smudging the mask in from the edges in
this way is very much easier than painting the mask, as the
smudging creates a natural, fading look that matches the
growth style of the grass.

2 The adjustment layer now has a mask that exactly matches the area outside the pot – so far, we'll see no difference. But when we switch to the Smudge tool, we can brush in the mask beneath the pot so that it hides the pot, giving the impression of grass growing up in front of it.

3 Experiment with changing brush size and pressure on the Smudge tool, dragging large clumps and individual blades up over the pot. All we're doing, of course, is hiding the pot by smudging the layer mask on the adjustment layer beneath it.

HOT TIP

The technique here works well for grass; but if we want to bury our object in a different surface, such as sand or snow, we'll need a slightly different technique. Rather than using the Smudge tool, use a soft-edged brush, but set the mode of the brush to Dissolve: this will create a granulated, speckled effect. To soften the effect, apply a little Gaussian Blur after painting the mask.

5 We now need to add some shading, both to the pot and the background. Make a new layer above the pot, grouped with it; set the mode of this layer to Multiply. Now sample a dark color from inside the pot, and use a soft-edged brush to paint shadows on the lower edges.

6 Finally, make a new layer above the grass. This is where we'll paint the shadows cast by the pot. Use a soft-edged brush again, with black as the foreground color: set the brush to a low opacity, and build up the shadow in small stages until it looks convincing.

On golden pond

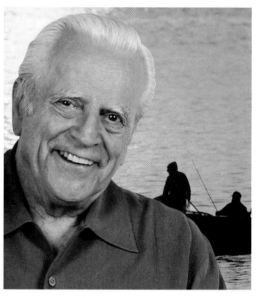

BLENDING TWO IMAGES TOGETHER is a technique that has many uses. Here, we'll look at a specialized use: making a composite of a man with his favorite hobby.

It's a technique that's reminiscent of the poster for the Henry Fonda movie, *On Golden Pond* – and that's why we've chosen this particular subject.

Blending the portrait into the background is straightforward enough, using the techniques outlined earlier in this chapter. But what makes this image work is blending the color as well, rather than simply relying on the colors in the original pictures. This is the secret to create a montage that looks unified, rather than two disparate elements.

1 Having chosen our background, the next step is to place our figure in front of it. Since he's the main figure in our composition, make him as large as possible within the frame, while leaving space top right for a caption.

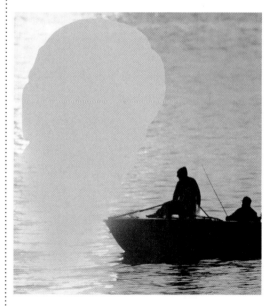

4 By default, a Color Fill adjustment layer comes out as black. Changing this to a warm orange better suits the background. As we can see, because the adjustment layer is grouped with the figure, it only shows up where it overlaps the man.

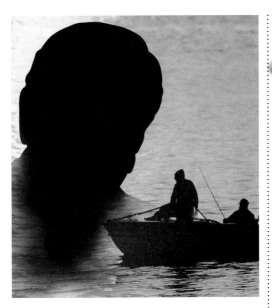

2 To fade him out, use the layer mask technique described earlier in this chapter: make a new Brightness/Contrast adjustment layer behind him, and group him with it; then paint in black on the mask to hide the layer, and paint in white to reveal it again.

3 At the end of the previous step, our image was working well as a composition: but the color didn't match the warm orange glow of the background. Create a new Color Fill adjustment layer using the pop-up menu at the bottom of the Layers palette, and group it with the figure layer.

5 In order to be able to see the man through the Color Fill, we need to change the layer's mode from Normal to Multiply. Now we can see the man clearly, and the color is having its effect. But it's much too strong: we need to lower the opacity of the layer.

6 Taking the opacity of the Color Fill layer down to 50% gives us the effect we want. He now has a coloring that matches the background far more closely: the two separate images are now unified into a single montage that works as a whole.

HOT TIP

By creating a layer mask in step 2, rather than simply erasing the figure around the boat, we have the flexibility we need to move him around and adjust the mask as required. It's important that the man doesn't hide the prow of the boat, for example; but it needs to wrap around it smoothly. This would be hard to achieve by simply erasing parts of the layer.

Part of the scene

BIG KIDS, LITTLE KIDS: how about giant kids? It's easy to turn a straightforward photograph into a King Kong creation by simply changing the background and adding a plane or two.

But we can go further than this. Placing a child in front of a scene may be the first step, but it's a long way from the finished montage. The trick is to bring picture elements from the background in front of any people or objects we've placed in the scene. By doing this, we're integrating our placed items in such a way as to make them appear to be genuinely part of the background, rather than merely floating on top. It makes all the difference between a straightforward montage, and a truly compelling scene.

1 We've placed the girl on the view of New York, and her feet fit neatly into the space in front of the buildings: the toy plane has been added to give her something to look at. But we can integrate her into the scene better than this.

4 In the last step, we left part of the girl's shoe showing beneath the new buildings layer, so we need to move her up. Judge where she fits best within this scene, positioning her so that her feet seem to be firmly planted behind the buildings.

2 Hide the girl's layer, and make a selection of the two buildings in the middle. With straight edges such as this, the Polygonal Lasso tool works best: you can also hold **alt** with the regular Lasso to trace straight lines.

3 Make the buildings into a new layer using **ctrl J** and move this layer above the girl's layer, so that she appears behind the buildings. She now looks like she's in the middle of the buildings.

HOT TIP

This trick of moving background elements to the front will help in just about any kind of montage. If there aren't any suitable background objects that can be 'promoted' in this way, then create your own: an out-of-focus bush, for example, can help an outdoor montage to look that much more realistic.

5 To integrate her further, we need to add some shadows. First, on a new layer, paint shadows beneath her foot on the ground below. Then make another layer just above the girl, grouped with her layer; paint shadows here on her leg, as if the building is adding shading to it.

6 Finally, we can move the plane so it's right in her line of sight. Also, by positioning it slightly in front of her hand, we further help to create the illusion that she's really standing in the middle of down town New York, batting away an attacking air force.

Polaroid style photos

POLAROID INSTANT CAMERAS may be somewhat out of favor since digital photography became so accessible, but the familiar shape of the photos they produce remains a popular way of framing images; particularly if you're looking to create a retro theme.

The following tutorial serves not only to explain the steps to create a great Polaroid effect, it also demonstrates the use of clipping groups to crop a photo down to fit the frame; this gives us the freedom to position, scale and rotate the image within the window before commiting to any permanent changes.

1 Begin by creating a new layer. Use the Rectangular Marquee **M** to mark out the shape of the frame. Fill the selection with white; this, of course, makes it difficult to see so we've colored the background, you could also turn the background layer off. Press **ctrl D** to deselect.

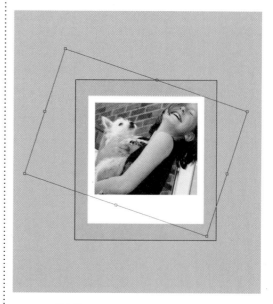

4 Press **ctrl T** to enter Free Transform, the image is quite large so you'll need to zoom out to see the whole of the bounding box. Now you can scale and rotate the photo within the frame – remember to keep the proportions constrained so it doesn't become distorted.

2 Draw an almost square selection inside the frame; offset it towards the top. Press *ctrl* *Shift* *J* to cut the section away to a new layer. Now drag its thumbnail down beneath the original layer in the Layers palette. I've made it clearer by filling it with gray.

3 Bring in your photo either by dragging the image into the document with the Move tool or by copying and pasting it. Make sure it's between the two sections of the frame. Press *ctrl* *G* to group the photo layer with the window backing; the remainder of the image is hidden.

5 Polaroid photos are thicker than normal prints so we need to give ours a bit of substance: click the Frame layer's thumbnail to make it active, now apply the Simple Inner Bevel. The default is far too large so double-click the style indicator and adjust the bevel's size.

6 To finish off the effect some texture has been applied to the frame using the Texturizer filter. Setting the texture to canvas with a very low relief gives us a rough but subtle effect, breaking up the solid white. A text layer has also been added; that's why the extra space is there, after all.

HOT TIP

You don't, of course, have to leave the Polaroid image square on the page once it's complete: multi-select the component layers (or link them if you have an older version of the program) and use free transform to make further changes. This way you still have the option to edit the text or adjust the photo a little. We've also placed a shadow beneath to add a sense of depth; see Chapter 5 for more on creating shadows.

Spectacular fireworks

FIREWORK DISPLAYS ARE FANTASTIC
to watch but notoriously difficult to
photograph, especially when there are other
elements in the scene to consider; the camera
has to be perfectly steady to prevent the
foreground from becoming horribly blurred –
not to mention the problem of timing the shot
to capture the moment at its best.

With Elements, of course, we can add our
own pyrotechnic delights. Although merging
something as complex as fireworks into a photo
might seem like an arduous task, it's surprisingly
simple: using a blend mode to knock out the
dark areas allowing the backround to show
through enables us to place them into the scene
precisely where we want them.

1 We've placed our first firework into the scene which has,
of course, hidden most of the background. There's far
too much going on to be able to select it or mask it out, and
lowering the opacity would cause it to become washed out.

4 The firework is too large so press **ctrl** **T** to invoke Free
Transform, now you can position and scale the firework
down so it fits into the scene – remember to hold **Shift** to
ensure the image remains in proportion.

2 The layer's background is almost black so we can use the Screen blend mode to filter it out leaving just the bright areas of the firework visible. This gives us an almost perfect result with no harsh contrasting edges.

3 We can see the backround is still visible against the original photo. Open the Levels dialog *ctrl* *L* and drag the shadow slider in from the left a little; you'll see the light area at the bottom begin to disappear.

5 We still have a problem: parts of the firework are in front of the tower when it should, of course, be behind. This is easily resolved by erasing, or better still, masking out the unwanted areas.

6 We've placed some additional fireworks to balance the image. Whilst we could have filled more of the sky, in this instance, we want to complement the scene, rather than totally drawing focus from it.

HOT TIP

If you're creating your firework display over a scene with an expanse of water or another shiny surface, you'll need to remember to add a suitable reflection for the fireworks as well. See Chapter 10 For more details.

Digital cameras

BEING ELEMENTS USERS, it's likely that you'll already have a camera of some type, even if it's not digital. You may, however, be looking to buy your first, or upgrade from your current model; and with so many different cameras on the market, choosing the right one can be a difficult decision. There are many factors to take into consideration and they are largely based on how much you intend to use it and for what purpose; you don't really want to be carrying huge amounts of equipment around with you if you're only interested in taking the occasional snapshot and similarly, if you're a keen photographer, you might be disappointed with the lack of features on a smaller model.

There are three main types of digital camera: let's begin with the compact models. Firstly, small is not necessarily a sacrifice in quality or features. Even at entry level, most start at 3 megapixels (Mp) which will give you a perfect quality 7"x5" print and a reasonable one at Letter or A4 size. Some have a fixed lens whilst others offer a moderate amount of optical zoom – don't fall for the digital zoom gimmick, though, the results are often lower quality because the image is enlarged by the software in the camera, and not by the lens. The features vary from set point-and-shoot modes to a reasonable amount of manual control, depending on the model.

Next in line are the mid-range cameras, sometimes referred to as prosumer (from professional-consumer). These are bulkier than the compacts but are generally higher quality having larger image sensors and more manual control of the settings. The lenses are larger with a good zoom factor; again, many still include the digital zoom feature in an attempt to make the package more attractive to the buyer.

Finally, we have the DSLR (Digital Single Lens Reflex) cameras: these are the most expensive, and largest, but do give the best image definition: most producing photos that can be printed at A3 with no degradation. They have the same control features as their film-based brethren and their lenses are interchangeable, many share the same mounts as their analogue predecessors, giving you the option of using your existing ones, if you choose the same manufacturer.

It's worth noting that when it comes to the resolution of a camera, bigger isn't necessarily better, especially on the compact cameras which use a smaller sensor; the receptors need to be more tightly packed and the definition of the image can suffer as a result. For most purposes anything between 3 and 7 megapixels is sufficient. Professional DSLRs tend to start at 6Mp and can go as high as 20Mp or more but you'll be paying out serious money at that level.

Once you've decided on the type of camera, you then need to choose the specific make and model: this can be another minefield, of course, and it's certainly a good idea to read reviews, both in magazines and online. There are two websites well worth visiting: **www.dpreview.com** and **www.stevesdigicams.com**; both offer highly in-depth information about almost every camera currently available – and sometimes advanced previews of the latest technology, as well as archives of the older models too.

From a photo-montage perspective, having a good camera certainly helps when it comes to sourcing images for your artwork. We'll talk about stock libraries elsewhere in the book and whilst you're almost certain to find the image you need on at least one of the sites, there's still no substitute for taking your own; you are in full control of the pictures and can get just the right angle and distance to suit your needs. You can create your own library of images, especially if you have a camera that you can carry with you easily at all times, that way you'll always be ready to capture those interesting scenes and textures. You can also set up a small home-studio for photographing smaller objects, either by buying a dedicated light box and lamps or, if you're feeling particularly adventurous, you could build your own – there are numerous websites with instructions on how to do this.

You might even consider uploading your own images to one of the many free stock libraries and add to the constantly growing resources. You may think that your contributions will be just a drop in a very large ocean but you may just provide someone with a picture of something nobody else has. If your pictures are of high enough quality you could subscribe to one of the micro-stock websites such as **www.istockphoto.com** or **www.shutterstock.com**. You never know, you may start earning some extra money from it, especially if you sign up with a lot of different ones. There's always the excitement of seeing one or more of your pictures in use on someone's website or in a book such as this, perhaps.

■ The Palace of Westminster is one of London's best-loved and most-photographed attractions. But the dull gray sky that's almost as much a London landmark makes the whole image look dull. How much better when we substitute a blue sky with fluffy clouds. It isn't hard to do, even though that tree may look fiddly.

elements 6

4

Image adjustments

DIGITAL CAMERAS are the best gadget the Elements user can own. But even the best camera can't produce sunny skies on an overcast day, or make snow from thin air, or change the color of a car. Fortunately, we have a solution.

Elements allows us to make any changes we like to an image: literally anything we can imagine can be changed within a single image. We can turn silver into gold, alter the time of day, and give the impression of speed.

But we can also enhance our images without adding anything new. Got a dull, lifeless photograph? We'll see how to liven it up in just a few steps – and how to recover apparently lost information from shadows and burnt-out highlights.

Adjusting images with Levels

1 When we open the Levels dialog using `ctrl L`, all the sliders are in their starting position: the black and white triangles on the extreme left and right respectively, and the gray triangle in the middle.

ELEMENTS INCLUDES SEVERAL METHODS for adjusting the brightness, contrast and tonal range in images. By far the most powerful – and the most versatile – is Levels, which gives a large degree of control over your pictures. Getting to grips with Levels will mean you're able to fine-tune your images to get perfect results.

The Levels dialog is in three parts: the histogram, the graph which shows the spread of tones in the image; the Input Levels, which allows you to adjust highlights, shadows and midtones; and the Output Levels, which controls the final brightness and contrast of the finished image.

4 Dragging the center gray slider will affect the midtone values. Here, dragging the slider to the left brightens the image, without changing the brightest and darkest areas.

7 Levels also gives access to the individual red, green and blue channels, using the pop-up menu. Here, dragging the midtone on the red channel to the right reduces the total amount of red.

2 Dragging the small white triangle in the Input section to the left will brighten the image overall. Similarly, dragging the black triangle to the right will darken it.

3 A good way to balance an image is to drag the black and white triangles so they touch the extreme edges of the histogram. This gives the image the full tonal range and makes it much crisper.

5 Dragging the black Output triangle to the right makes the image brighter; dragging the white triangle to the left would make the whole thing darker. Moving either will reduce image contrast.

6 Pressing the Auto button will examine the histogram and produce what Elements thinks is the best result. Often, pressing this button can produce a marked improvement at a stroke.

8 When we drag either the black or the white Input triangles, the middle gray triangle moves with it to remain spaced half way between light and dark.

9 By dragging this midtone gray marker towards the light end, we can produce a strong, graphic effect.

HOT TIP

If you make a mistake and feel everything has gone horribly wrong, don't panic: press the Reset button to return the dialog to its original state.

You can use the three eyedropper tools to adjust the image automatically. With the black (left) dropper, click in the darkest part of the image; click the brightest with the white (right) dropper. Use the gray (center) dropper to click on a neutral gray in your image (if there is one), to color balance the image.

Shadows and highlights

Exposure is the one factor that photographers worry about more than any other. Professional photographers will always 'bracket' their exposures – that is, they'll take a range of exposures of the same image to make sure they've got the right one.

The real difficulty comes when we're faced with an image like this: a view through a window. In the image captured by the camera, above, we can see that the room itself is too dark (we can barely make out the blind texture among those deep shadows), while the view is so bleached out as to be wholly indistinct.

We can fix both of these problems in one go, with the Shadows/highlights adjustment. It's a hugely powerful tool, which can rescue even the most poorly exposed photographs.

1 After opening the image, go to Enhance > Lighting > Shadows/highlights, and the dialog above will appear. As long as the Preview button is checked, any changes you make here will be visible immediately in the image. The default setting for this adjustment is to Lighten Shadows by a value of 25% and, as we can see here, this setting manages to rescue some of the darker areas of the image. We can already see that there's a yellow pattern in the blind, for example.

2 That's not enough for our purposes. Let's increase the value significantly – here, we've dragged the slider to raise it to 80%. Now, the pattern and texture in the blind can be clearly seen. In addition, we can see that the dark field outside the window has now acquired some definition: the trees on the hill are now distinct from the plowed field in front of them.

3 Now let's turn our attention to the Highlights. As the image stands, the sky is greatly over-exposed. Dragging the Darken Highlights slider addresses this problem: the further to the right we drag it, the more detail we're able to see in the sky. We've dragged it here to a value of 70%, and this means that the clouds now stand out from the sky behind them.

4 Although we could stop there, it's worth looking at the final slider – Midtone Contrast. Generally, we'd welcome contrast, as it provides definition within the image. Here, though, the result of tweaking both the shadows and the highlights has resulted in a window frame that's so well defined that it overpowers the view through it. By lowering the midtone contrast we take out a little of that over-defined molding, drawing the eye through the window to the view instead.

Bee flat to bee sharp

W E ALWAYS STRIVE to get the best possible images but sometimes, even with the best equipment, we can end up with an image that is slightly soft.

In our example the combination of the extreme close-up and the bee's movement has resulted in a less defined photo. There is, of course, no way to get a clearer image once it's been taken but we can enhance it to give the impression of it being a lot sharper. We'll have a look at two different sharpening methods here; each providing a slightly different effect.

Rather than working directly on the image, however, we'll use a grayscale copy and blend it with the original; this way we have far greater control over the final effect.

These effects can, of course, be applied to any image, regardless of its original clarity; by reducing the amount of adjustment we can give a photo some added pop.

1 Here's our slightly soft photo in need of a little attention. We're not going to work on the image directly so the first step is to duplicate the background layer. Both techniques require a grayscale layer so we need to desaturate the layer by pressing `ctrl` `Shift` `U`.

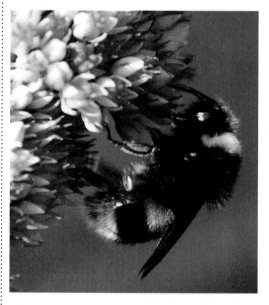

4 Without adjustment applied we can overlay it onto our original image: set the blend mode to Soft Light, it's looking a lot sharper whilst retaining much of its tonal qualities and color balance, something that could be affected if we'd applied the effect directly to the image.

2 For the first technique we'll use the Unsharp Mask adjustment. This can be found at the bottom of the Enhance menu – in previous versions it can be found in the Filter menu under Sharpen. The dialog may look a little daunting but it's surprisingly straightforward.

3 The default settings are fairly tame and have little effect on our image. Drag the Amount slider to the right; don't be afraid to increase it higher than you would normally, it won't look as severe when we blend it with the original; in this case we raised it to 350%.

HOT TIP

There is no right or wrong way of sharpening; the method used depends greatly on the image itself. Some photos may require an all-over effect, whereas others may just need their edges enhanced. Because we're applying the adjustment to a layer we can experiment with different blend modes and opacities; even combine the techniques. At worst, all we would need to do is create a new effect layer and reapply the adjustment.

5 The second technique makes use of a little-known filter called High Pass; this resides in the Filter menu under Other. There is only one slider and, unlike Unsharp Mask, we only need to make a small adjustment to achieve good results – we've used a setting of 3 pixels here.

6 As before, we need to change the blend mode, this time, set it to Hard Light. This is a more subtle effect than the Unsharp Mask version, concentrating more on the edges than the entire image but still gives superb results and leaves the original color almost unchanged.

63

All that glitters...

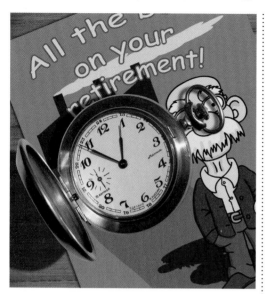

CHANGING A SILVER OBJECT to gold is not a difficult task. The two metals are very similar. They both have the same specular properties; the way light is reflected back from their surfaces (once polished, of course). Silver has a high content of blue giving it its colder appearance. Gold, on the other hand, is predominantly red and green. It's simply a matter of adjusting the hues to give us the familiar warm color. Although you might be tempted to use a Hue/Saturation adjustment, we'll use the Levels dialog. By working with the color channels individually, we have far greater control.

1 Here's our silver watch. The face has been cut away from the rest of the image and placed on a separate layer. We only want to color the body, after all.

3 Now switch to the red channel. This time increase the amount by moving the mid-tone slider across to the left. As you can see, our watch is now looking much more valuable. It's still a little dull though.

2 Make sure the body layer is active by clicking its thumbnail in the Layers palette. Open the Levels dialog by pressing *ctrl* **L**. Select the Blue Channel from the drop down menu. Move the mid-tone slider towards the right. As the blue is subtracted from the image, the color becomes noticeably greener and much closer to gold.

4 Switch back to the composite RGB view. Drag the Highlight and Shadow sliders a little way toward the middle. This gives us a richer tone to the color as well as giving the impression the metal is much shinier.

HOT TIP

You can also select the individual channel views from the keyboard. Holding *ctrl* and **1 2** or **3** will switch between the red, green and blue channels respectively. Press *ctrl* and the ~ (tilde) key to return to the composite RGB view – not the more logical 0, as you might think. This, of course, is the reserved shortcut for the Fit on Screen view mode.

The perfect respray

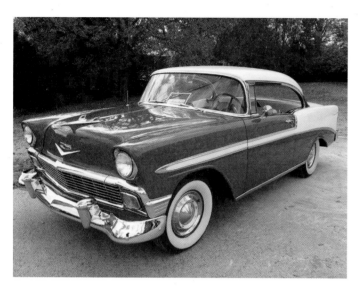

THERE ARE NUMEROUS WAYS to change the color of an object. Most, however, are designed to affect the entire image. We could, of course, use the selection tools to isolate the parts we need to work on. This is a time consuming practice and often more trouble than it's worth.

For tricky jobs, such as this car with all that complex trim, by far the best method is to use the Replace Color tool. With this we can selectively alter the hue, saturation and lightness of an area without the need to separate it from the rest of the image.

IMAGE: PEGGY S. SIMONI/MORGEFILE.COM

1 Press **ctrl J** to duplicate the background layer. Open the dialog by going to Enhance > Adjust Color > Replace Color. The white area in the preview shows the selected area after clicking a section of the car's body. We've set the Fuzziness to its maximum for now, we'll adjust it later.

2 Instead of applying the new color straight away, we've lowered the saturation completely; this shows up the more subtle shades of red not included initially. We can add these areas to the selection by holding **Shift** and clicking them with the eyedropper.

3 We've isolated all of the car's color but we now have a problem: looking at the preview, a large amount of unwanted areas have been included from the rest of the image. This is where we'll use the Fuzziness setting to fine-tune the result.

4 By gradually lowering the Fuzziness value we can see the selection start to tighten up in the preview. Some of the previously selected color will begin to reappear. Zoom in a little and start to add these back in. If necessary, adjust the Fuzziness a little more until you have a good balance.

5 Now we can add the new color by raising the Saturation and altering the Hue to the desired shade. As we began by duplicating the image we can simply erase the unwanted areas, such as the for sale sign in the window and the trees in the background, to let the original show through.

6 You may notice there are still places where the original hue remains. Often this will be noticeable in the highlights and reflections. As a final touch, grab a soft brush. Set its Blend Mode to Color. Now you can carefully paint over these areas with the target color.

HOT TIP

The Fuzziness setting of the dialog works in a similar way to the tolerance feature of tools such the Magic Wand. By increasing the value, Elements will select a greater tonal range of the chosen color. This can be used to avoid harsh lines where two hues meet. It's rarely possible to achieve a perfect result with no excess areas affected, if we keep refining the balance by adjusting the fuzziness and adding in small amounts to the selection we can keep problems to a minimum.

Changing skies

1 Select the Background Eraser tool, and change its limits from Contiguous to Discontiguous. A Tolerance setting of around 40% works well for this plain sky. Click and drag around the tower to delete the background, but be sure not to let the crosshair stray onto the building.

THE BACKGROUND ERASER is a fantastic tool for removing areas of similar color. It's the second of the Eraser tools, and it works by sampling the color beneath the crosshair, and deleting all the pixels of that color within the radius of the brush. Here, we're going to use it to erase all the sky from this photograph of London's Houses of Parliament, and replace it with a more dramatic sky.

Although we could select and delete much of the background using the Magic Wand tool, that won't select inside fiddly areas such as the tree: this is where the 'discontiguous' setting of the Background Eraser comes in handy, as we'll see in this example.

Before we start with this tool, it's important to duplicate the layer you're going to work on, hiding the original so there's always a copy we can return to later.

4 Continue erasing all the sky within the image, varying the size of the brush as you need to. Don't worry if some areas of the picture are erased that shouldn't be; we can get those back later. For now, concentrate on getting rid of all that sky.

2 When we move into the tree area, we get a problem. Once the crosshair touches the branches, that's the color that's sampled – and so that's the area that is deleted. We need to find another way to remove the sky in there. Undo that step, and we'll try again.

3 Make the Eraser brush size much larger – we've used a 175 pixel brush here. Click on a clear area of blue sky within the tree branches, and all the sky within the radius of the brush will be deleted. Make sure you don't click on the branches by accident.

5 When we now bring in a new sky layer behind the buildings, we can see a few mistakes: the clock face has been erased, and we can see the new sky through it, and the same applies to one or two parts of the buildings. Just as well we were working on a copy of the layer!

6 Make selections around the missing building parts, using the Lasso tool. Now return to the original (hidden) layer, and press *ctrl* *J* to make a new layer from the selection. Move this layer above the clouds layer, and the image is complete.

HOT TIP

There are several settings for this tool. The first is choosing between Contiguous and Discontiguous: the former will find edges, and the latter will look inside bounded regions such as the branches of the tree. The Tolerance setting depends on how uniform the background is. The higher the Tolerance, the wider the range of deleted colors will be. It's a matter of judgment for each image individually; start with a setting of around 50%, and increase or decrease it as needed.

0–60 in ten minutes

IF YOU'VE EVER TRIED TO PHOTOGRAPH a moving object such as a car, you may have found the results disappointing. When cameras are set to automatic mode they have a nasty habit of removing the action from the image by freezing the motion.

Fortunately for us it's not difficult to put the drama back, or, as we'll be doing with the image above, creating movement from a stationary image. We'll see two different ways of doing this: the first mimics the use of a slow shutter speed by blurring the object in front of a static background. The second method is the opposite effect: the car remains still whilst the background is blurred. This would be the result of panning – the result of following the subject's movement with the camera whilst taking the shot.

1 The first task is to isolate the car from its background. A combination of the the Magnetic Lasso and the Selection Brush is best for doing this. The latter being used to tidy up the tricky areas of low contrast. Copy the car to its own layer by pressing **ctrl J**.

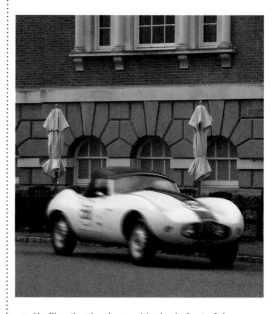

4 You'll notice there's some blurring in front of the car as well as behind; most prominently around the tires and far right of the bodywork. This, of course, wouldn't happen unless it was being vigorously shaken. Select a large, soft eraser. Use the edge to carefully remove the unwanted areas.

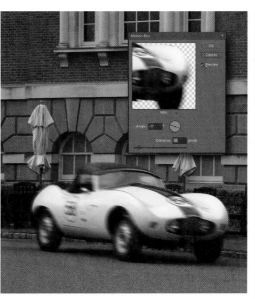

2 One common trait of speed is the wheels. Use the Elliptical Marquee to select one of the wheels (not the tire). Open the Radial Blur filter, set the method to Spin. The amount depends on the required effect; we've used 25 here. Deslect *ctrl* *D* and repaeat for the other wheel.

3 First we'll create the effect of the car zooming past. Open the Motion Blur filter – make sure Preview is enabled. Start by setting the distance. Keep this subtle to avoid it looking too much like a cartoon. Now adjust the angle to suit the direction of the car's movement.

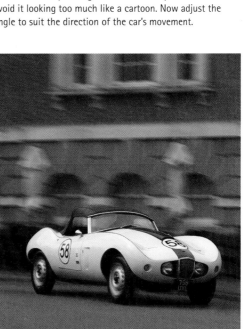

5 Here's a different approach. Make the background layer active. Apply the Motion Blur filter; as before, set the distance and angle. You can add a slightly heavier effect this time. Once again there are some unwanted areas. We'll deal with those next.

6 Select the Clone Stamp. Using a small soft tip, go around the car painting over the sections of where the overspill is most pronounced. Finally, switch back to the car layer. Use a small eraser to remove the windows to reveal the blurred background of the original image.

HOT TIP

When you're cloning in parts of a blurred image you can often afford to be a little less precise than you would be where the detail is visible. As long as there are no obvious areas where there's a repeating pattern or misalignment, a little artistic licence will most likely go unnoticed.

71

Sunset silhouette

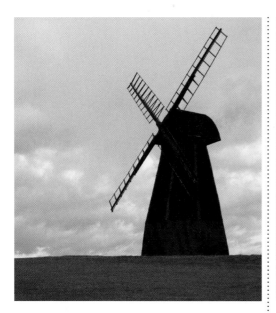

ARLIER IN THIS CHAPTER we looked at replacing a washed out sky with a more impressive one. Simply changing the existing sky isn't always enough, however: depending on the type of scene we want to produce, we will often need to adjust the foreground to match. We'll demonstrate this by transforming our uninspiring photo of a windmill into a lovely evening silhouette.

As the sun sets its light changes, becoming a richer, more orange tone which, in turn. affects the scene's colors. We can mimic this by adjusting the levels of the image; it's important not to darken the subject too far, we still want to be able to see some detail.

Producing images in this way not only lets us rescue dull photos, it also allows us to create difficult to capture or sometimes impossible views: with Elements, the sun will always be just where we want it.

1 Here we've duplicated the background layer and removed the sky: the Background Eraser made easy work of the fiddly areas of the sail frames. Our sunset image is then placed on a layer behind. As you can see, it's not looking particularly convincing at this stage.

4 We need a shadow to complete the scene: load the windmill layer's selection. Only the outline of the windmill is needed so grab the Polygonal Lasso tool, hold *Shift* *alt* to switch to intersect mode and draw across its base, follow on with a loose selection around the rest.

2 Make the windmill layer active and load its selection by holding **ctrl** and clicking its thumbnail in the Layers palette. Create a Levels adjustment layer; the selected area becomes a mask so the changes we make will only affect the foreground image.

3 Drag the midtone slider across to the right to make the tones richer and darker. Increase the Shadows slightly and bring the Highlights up a little by dragging the slider to the left. Select the red channel **ctrl 1**. Drag the midtones a little to the left to deepen the red hue.

5 Create a new layer above the adjustment layer, now fill the selection with black. Deselect by pressing **ctrl D** and enter free transform mode **ctrl T**. Distort the shadow into position by holding **ctrl** and dragging the corner handles – you'll need to zoom out to stretch it past the bottom edge.

6 The shadow is too harsh so we'll use a small amount of Gaussian Blur to soften the edges and lower the opacity a little so it's not completely black against the background. As a final step, we've used the Ripple filter to add the effect of the shadow falling across the uneven grass.

HOT TIP

It's often not possible to remove all traces of the background, particularly in small, intricate areas of the photo. When placed against a darker image these lighter areas can show up as a halo around the isolated object. We could zoom in with a smaller eraser to tidy it up but this is fiddly and we could end up removing parts of the image we meant to keep. Instead, use the Burn tool to darken and blend in the offending areas; this can also be used to paint over any brighter elements in the scene that the Levels adjustment doesn't affect.

73

That's snow business

WE DON'T SEEM TO GET THE SAME amount of snow as we did in years gone by; whilst some people would say this is a good thing, it is a shame not to see the stunning white backdrop blanketing the streets and countryside, it does make a particularly great photo opportunity, after all.

This is not a problem for the montage artist, however. With a little effort we can take almost any scene and add a little wintry magic; what's more is we will never have to worry about the fresh snowfall being disturbed before we get our shot.

This technique can be used to make great seasonal greetings cards, calendars or just to create a scene you may never see — snow in Egypt, perhaps?

1 Here's our charming Dickensian scene ready for a fresh snowfall. We'll begin by creating a new layer `ctrl` `alt` `Shift` `N`, which will be where we'll add the areas of built up snow.

2 Set the foreground color to white and grab the Brush tool `B`. Select a small, hard tip and start to paint where the snow would lay: on the arch over the door, and so on. Remember to leave a slight overhang.

6 Switch back to the main snow layer. Add a small amount of monochromatic Gaussian Noise to give it some texture, around 7% is enough, we don't want it too grainy.

7 Grab the Burn tool `O`, use a small soft tip set to a low exposure to paint in some random shading on the snow; particularly the underside to give it some thickness.

3 Carry on adding in areas of snow: on the railings – create small peaks around the spikes, and on top of the tree, of course. Being rounded you should paint this to around a third of the way down.

4 Create a new layer above the snow layer. Set the Brush's blend mode to Dissolve and lower the opacity to around 20%. Paint in some small areas of powdery snow on the walls, the bench, tree and on the door.

5 Set the brush mode back to normal and raise the opacity back to 100%. Paint in the small area of ground by the door. Now add a tiny amount of Gaussian Blur to soften it giving the effect of a light dusting.

8 Create a layer at the top of the stack. Fill this with black and add a large amount of noise; around 100 pixels. Apply some Gaussian Blur, we want to achieve a soft mottled effect.

9 Open the Levels adjustment, bring the white point up to the base of the peak on the right hand side. Now drag the black point up toward it; this creates our falling snow effect.

10 Set the blend mode to Screen to hide the black, leaving just the flakes visible. Lower the saturation of the background layer; snowy days tend to wash out color of the scene.

HOT TIP

For this image one falling snow layer is enough as we are quite close to the buildings. If we could see further into the distance, we could add the illusion of depth to the scene by duplicating the layer, scaling it down and tiling it. By doing this several times it appears that the snow is getting smaller as it extends away from us.

75

But is it art?

THE ART WORLD CAN BE A FICKLE and sometimes intimidating place. Whilst the majority of its denizens are more than happy to welcome new concepts such as digital art with open arms, there will doubtless be the old-school stalwarts who balk at the very notion of the capability of something as utilitarian as a computer being the medium for any kind of creative expression. This is nothing new, of course: photography also received the same amount of steely renunciation when people started using it as anything other than a functional method of preserving images of people and places. It took the work of the late, great photographer Ansel Adams and others like him to prove that the photograph could have just as much visual impact and provide the same aesthetic pleasure as paintings by the old masters.

Unfortunately, as with many things, there can also be a degree of fighting within the ranks as well. There are those who frown upon certain aspects of digital art, such as photo-montage and 3D imagery, seeing it as compensation for lack of talent because it's not created from scratch, and often uses other people's work as a constituent. This is, of course, a ludicrous way of thinking. Nobody thinks to question the validity of art-forms such as decorative floristry, which quite obviously doesn't necessarily require the flowers to be grown by the artist beforehand; it is, after all, the end result that matters, and not how it was achieved.

Squabbling aside, one of the main accomplishments of the digital age is its ability to unlock and uncover artistic flair. We may shy away from trying out our ideas, often because we lack confidence in our abilities, believing that we'll make irreversible or costly mistakes. Another reason might be one of space and time, or the lack thereof: a studio requires a fair amount of working space and it's not always practical to set one up permanently; it can take a while to ready the materials and pack them away after a session, all of which does nothing to aid the creative process.

This is where computers come into their own. In general they're fairly self-contained, taking up only a small proportion of space and they can be ready for action in just a few minutes. What really sets them apart, however, is their forgiving nature: make a mistake on canvas and you've got a fair amount of tidying up ahead of you – at worst you'll have to paint over it and start afresh, which is demoralizing to say the least.

Working digitally is a different matter entirely, with technologies such as layers, non-destructive adjustments and styles; and not forgetting the trusty undo function, you can afford to think more freely in the knowledge that you have these safety-nets to catch you, should you falter and lose your artistic balance.

It's not all plain sailing, of course. The standard equipment that comes with a PC, usually a mouse, is great for moving the cursor around the screen to point at links in web pages, menus and highlight passages of text in a word-processor, but not so good for creating a masterpiece. Imagine trying to draw with a pencil shaped like a soap bar: it's not impossible, but it can be awkward and become uncomfortable after a while. If you're considering any kind of digital art as a serious hobby or even as a profession then a graphics tablet is an essential purchase. They can take a while to get used to, however; there's often a period where hand-eye coordination causes problems — we are usually more accustomed to looking directly at what we're drawing, rather than away to a screen. Once you have overcome this, it's unlikely you'll want to stop using it: outlining and selections can be achieved in half the time and you can really see the difference with the painting tools. Using a pressure-sensitive device makes shading an absolute delight, rather than the constant size and opacity changing nightmare it once was. Many tablets have configurable buttons on the stylus which can be set to emulate key-presses; for example, you could set one up as the spacebar allowing you to pan around the image whilst zoomed in for close-up work. Some also have an eraser function when the stylus is flipped over which also saves time.

There are, of course, some things that even the most powerful computer technology can't provide you with: imagination and determination. You're on your own there, but without the constraints that may have been holding you back before, you're free to express yourself in whatever way you see fit. There is no rule book to abide by here, just do what seems good at the time.

Who knows, those images you had locked away in your head might be just what the art editor of a magazine is looking for, so get creating!

It's not difficult to create a simple montage like this one – a boy sitting on the White House lawn. But while he may be in the correct place, the image above looks unconvincing. By adding shadows, both on the boy and beneath him, we greatly increase the sense of realism, making it appear as if he was really photographed in this location.

5
Light and shade

WHEN WE COMBINE IMAGES from several different sources, we can scale them, rotate them and distort them to fit the space – but they still won't look quite right. In order to achieve a true realistic appearance, we need to add shadows. Whether they're cast on the ground, the wall or on other objects, it's shadows that will help your montages to work as complete images, and look less like obvious compositions.

Of course, there's a lot more to light and shade than just adding shadows. In this chapter we'll also look at how to make fire from scratch, how to add a spotlight effect to a stage curtain, and how to turn day into night.

Shadows on ground and wall

SHADOWS CAN MAKE THE DIFFERENCE between a convincing montage and one that looks like several images placed together. And yet shadows are often overlooked in the rush to get things done.

It's easy to make shadows on the wall and on the ground – easier still if the base of the wall is at right angles to the viewer, as it is here. The ball, the girl and the background are three separate layers, which makes it easy for us to place shadows between them.

We'll look at two different methods for creating shadows: the girl and the ball require different treatments to produce their effect.

1 Begin by loading up the girl as a selection by holding *ctrl* and clicking on her thumbnail in the Layers palette. Make a new layer, feather the selection using *ctrl* *alt* *D*, and fill with black. Deselect, move this layer behind the girl, and drag it out to the side.

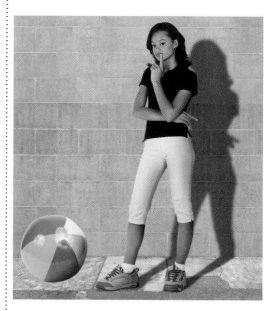

4 All we need to do now is to reduce the strength of this layer so we can see through it. We can change the opacity by dragging the slider at the top of the Layers palette; a simpler way is to use the number keys – *3* for 30%, *4* for 50%, and so on. We've used a 50% opacity.

2 Now make a rectangular selection of the shadow at about knee height. Enter Free Transform with **ctrl** **T**, and drag the top center handle down to meet the bottom of the wall. Then hold **ctrl** as you drag the bottom center handle to meet her feet.

3 With the floor section of the shadow complete, we can move on to the wall part. Select the remaining piece of shadow with the Marquee tool, and simply drag it down until it meets the ground. Stretch it vertically slightly if you need to.

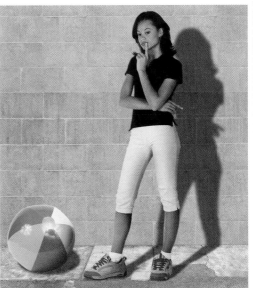

5 The ball's shadow requires a different treatment. As it's a spherical object, it will cast an elliptical shadow: so use the Elliptical Marquee tool, on a new layer, to make a selection. Feather it as before, and fill with black. Make sure it's behind the ball layer.

6 Lower the opacity of the ball shadow to match that of the girl, and then move it so that its position corresponds with the angle set by the girl's shadow. As it's a separate layer, it's easy to move and transform it until it looks exactly right.

HOT TIP

The distance of the shadow from the girl is determined by her distance from the wall: the closer she is to the wall, the closer her shadow will be.

Not all objects on the ground are as obliging as this ball: for more complex shapes, paint the shadow on a new layer with a soft edged brush, working at a low opacity to build it up in stages.

If you're working with a wall that isn't parallel to the bottom of the picture, you'll need a slightly different technique. In step 2, cut the bottom half of the shadow to a new layer; distort both parts, and erase any overlap.

81

Painting soft shadows

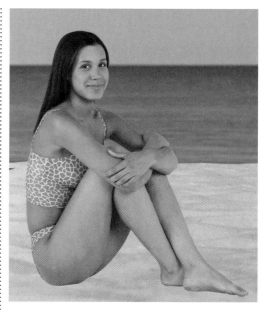

ON THE PREVIOUS PAGES we looked at how to create shadows cast on a wall and on the ground, by duplicating the figure and filling with black. But some kinds of shadow can't be created this easily: seated figures, such as this one, need shadows to be painted by hand.

As well as adding shadows beneath the figure, we need to add some shading to the figure itself in order for the effect to work properly. The technique we'll use here is more efficient than painting directly onto the figure, and gives us greater flexibility and accuracy.

1 When we place our figure of a seated girl onto this beach background, she looks as if she's hovering above the surface: we need to add shadows to place her more firmly on the ground.

4 We also need shadows on the girl herself, to make sense of those cast beneath her. Although we could paint directly onto her layer, here's a better method. First, hold **ctrl** and click on the thumbnail of the girl's layer in the Layers palette to load this area up as a selection.

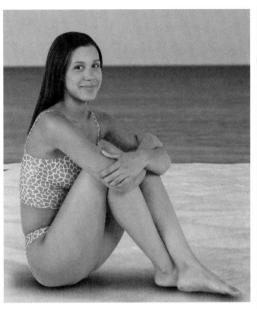

2 Begin by making a new layer between the girl and the background. Using a soft-edged brush set to an opacity of around 40%, paint the shadows beneath the places where she's touching the surface. By working at a low opacity, we can build the shadow up in stages.

3 Now switch to a larger, soft edged brush, and reduce the opacity of the brush still further. We can now paint the shadows cast by her body and her legs: they're fainter than those directly beneath the points of contact, and the lower opacity will help us achieve this effect.

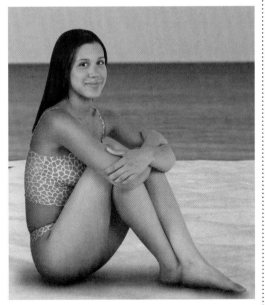

5 Make a new layer and, in the dialog that appears, make the mode of this layer Hard Light and set it to fill with a Hard Light neutral color (which is a mid-gray). Then inverse the selection using **ctrl Shift I** and delete the area outside her: here's how the layer would look if it were set to Normal.

6 When set to Hard Light, the gray is invisible. But when we use the Burn tool, set to a soft-edged brush, to paint on this layer, we can darken it up. Add shading to her undersides, beneath her legs and bottom, to link her shadow into the shadows we've already painted beneath her.

HOT TIP

The best way to paint shadows is to use a pressure sensitive graphics tablet. If you don't have one, then use a low opacity and build the shadow up in small stages. If the finished shadow looks too dark, then remember you can always lower the opacity of the shadow layer to reduce the effect.

83

Turning day into night

T AKING PHOTOS AT NIGHT generally
requires the use of a tripod to avoid shaky
or fuzzy images. You won't always have one
with you, especially if you're just out for the
day and happen to spot a scenic view such as
the quaint English pub in the above photo.
Whilst it's a great picture in its own right, it
probably looks equally as good after dark.

In the following tutorial we'll fast-forward
to a night view almost exclusively using
adjustment layers to create the effect. This way
we have total control over the look and feel
of the final image or take it back to daylight
whenever we wish.

1 Use the Magic Wand **W** to select the sky; hold **Shift** to
add the different sections together. Any stray areas can
be tidied with the Selection Brush or Lasso tools. Inverse the
selection **ctrl** **Shift** **I**. Now press **ctrl** **J** to create a copy of
the foreground.

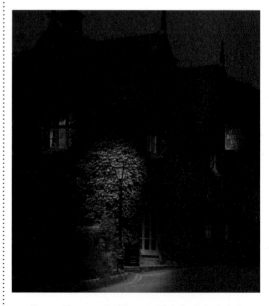

4 Now we'll create the lit areas. Click the Color layer's
mask thumbnail. Now select a soft brush set to a low
opacity and begin to paint in black over the areas where
light would fall: around the lamp and windows. This hides
the color layer to reveal the original daylight image beneath.

2 The next stage is to isolate the glass of the street lamp and the windows that will be lit. The Polygonal Lasso is best for this job: hold *alt* to switch to the Freehand Lasso to select the tricky areas around the leaves. Add a light feather to the selection and copy to a new layer.

3 Create a Levels adjustment layer between the building and the layer you just created, accept the defaults for now. Add a Solid Color layer above that. Select a midnight blue color, this will create the night effect. Set its blend mode to Multiply and drop the opacity to around 80%.

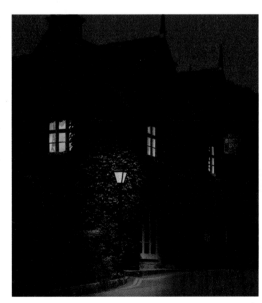

5 We need to adjust the lighting a little. It's too harsh for our image. Double-click the Layers adjustment layer to bring up its settings. Darken the shadows by dragging the left slider toward the middle. Add some warmth by raising the red channel's midtones and lowering the blue.

6 Create a new Color Fill layer above the windows. Choose a fairly deep orange hue, set the blend mode to Linear Dodge and drop the opacity to tone the effect down a little. Now press *ctrl* *G* to create a clipping group and restrict the color to the light sources.

Making fire

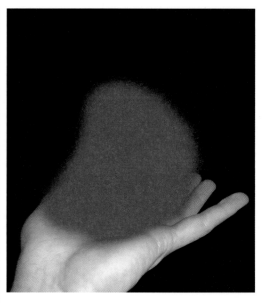

1 Begin by painting a blob, using a soft-edged brush, on a new layer. The shape and size don't matter that much at this stage, as we'll transform both later in the process; this is just the starting point.

ACCORDING TO LEGEND, it was Prometheus who brought fire to mankind – and suffered a particularly grisly fate as reward for his efforts.

Here's a method of creating fire that doesn't end up with us being chained to a rock and having our livers repeatedly pecked out by eagles. (Strange storytellers, the ancient Greeks.)

We'll create our fire from scratch, the only photograph being the hand we choose to place it on. Of course, you could set fire to anything – a house, a car, a landscape; whatever you choose, bear in mind that the effect will work very much better if you start with a black or very dark background. Flames rarely have the same impact on a bright summer's day.

This is the kind of image you can keep working at until the result looks exactly as you want it: there's a lot of fun to be had from continuously tweaking those flames.

4 We need a bright heart at the center of this flame. Using a soft edged brush, paint a yellow glow covering about a third of the flame area; then switch to white, and paint a much smaller blob of color right at the bottom. It's already starting to look quite flame like.

2 Use the Smudge tool, set to a strength of around 70% to 80%, to smudge that red blob into the beginnings of flame-like structures. Make sure the tool is not set to Sample All Layers, or you'll end up smudging the hand as well.

3 To make the basic texture, first lock the layer's transparency by clicking the Lock icon at the top of the Layers palette (or press ⬛). Set the foreground and background colors to red and yellow, and apply Filter > Render > Clouds.

5 Using the Smudge tool once more, tweak up that yellow and white into fire-like shapes, reaching up into the body of the flame. This is also a good time to darken the hand: open the Levels dialog, and drag the middle gray triangle to the right, about 80% of the way along.

6 Now unlock the transparency on the layer, and work on the flames with the Smudge tool once more. Switch between large and small brush sizes to work on large areas and details; remember, you can smudge down from outside the flame area, as well as up from the middle of it.

HOT TIP

Locking the transparency in step 3 allows us to apply the Clouds filter just to the flame area – otherwise, it would fill the whole canvas. We need to unlock it again in step 6, so that we can distort the flame layer. Getting from step 5 to step 6 took longer than the whole of the rest of the process: it's a slow and painstaking procedure to get this to look right. Don't rush it, and you'll be rewarded for your efforts.

Instant candlelight

E VEN THOUGH CANDLES have long been obsolete as a source of lighting, we still rely on them for the atmosphere they bring, for the sense of occasion they lend to any event.

On the previous pages, we looked at how to create a fireball. Making a single candle flame is a slightly different process, in that it's painted entirely 'by hand', using no filters.

This isn't a difficult procedure, but it can result in a spectacular image: the trick is to paint each stage slowly, building up the effect as we go along.

If you want to take it a step further and add smoke to your flame, you can see how it's done in *Smoke without Fire*, in Chapter 6.

1 Start by placing your candle on a dark background so the flames show up well. We've used a deep red curtain.

2 On a new layer, paint a rough shape in pale orange, using a soft-edged brush. Don't worry too much about the exact shape yet.

7 Continue smudging the top of the flame, perhaps with a smaller brush, until you're happy with the shape.

8 Changing the mode of the flame layer from Normal to Hard Light gives it added impact.

3 Use the Burn tool **O** set to Midtones, and darken the bottom of the flame around the wick to give the flame depth.

4 Switch to the Dodge tool, set to Highlights, and use it to brighten the center of the flame, turning it from orange to yellow.

5 Continue painting the flame in with the Dodge tool, until the center is a brilliant, glowing white (but don't overdo it).

6 Now use the Smudge tool **R**, with a large brush size, to twist the candle flame into a more appropriate shape.

HOT TIP

When we started to brighten the flame in step 4, we brought the yellow down into the orange a little way. Continuing with the Dodge tool in step 5 hardens the edge between the yellow and the orange, automatically producing the subtle glow effect we see at the base.

9 It's possible to create a huge variety of flame shapes by distorting the original painting with the Smudge tool – particularly handy when you want to make a row of candles. No need to paint each flame, just duplicate and smudge it.

10 For a stronger result, try painting a soft glow on a new layer behind the flame, using the same orange we started with (but at a low opacity). Darkening the background also draws attention to the flame itself.

Stage lighting

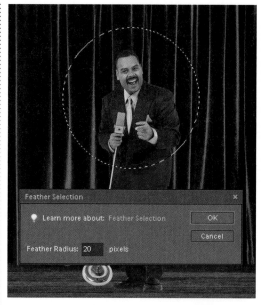

WE ALL WANT TO BE ON THE STAGE: now, thanks to Elements, we can easily achieve this ambition.

The trick to creating stage lighting is to think in reverse. You might imagine that the way to add a spotlight effect would be to place a bright disk over the affected area: but you'd be wrong. Rather than adding light to the spotlit region, we'll subtract it elsewhere – in the form of a shadow with a circular hole in it.

And just for good measure, let's add a glow from the spotlight just out of shot, and a shadow cast on the curtain behind.

1 Begin by making a circular selection: hold **Shift** as you trace with the Elliptical Marquee tool to make a perfect circle. Now use **ctrl** **alt** **F** to bring up the Feather dialog, and add a large feather radius – about 20 pixels is sufficient for this task.

4 Now for the visible light. Make a rectangular selection and feather it as before, with a feather radius of 20 pixels. Choose a very pale yellow color and, on a new layer, use the Gradient tool set to Foreground to Transparent to drag from left to right, making a faded glow.

2 Make a new layer, and inverse the selection by pressing **ctrl** **Shift** **I**. Now, everything except the feathered circle is selected. Press **D** to make the foreground color black, then **alt** **Backspace** to fill the selection with the foreground color.

3 At the end of the previous step, the shadow was so strong that we were unable to see anything through it. Lower the opacity of the shadow layer, either by dragging the slider at the top of the Layers palette, or by pressing a number key: pressing **7** gives an opacity of 70%.

5 Use Free Transform (**ctrl** **T**) to rotate and distort the glow so that it comes in from the top left of the picture. If you hold **ctrl** **alt** **Shift** while you drag one of the corner points you'll produce a perspective distortion, which will give the impression of the beam getting larger.

6 Finally, add the shadow behind the man. Load up his selection by holding **ctrl** as you click on his thumbnail in the Layers palette; then use the technique described earlier in this chapter to make a shadow that sits on the curtain behind him, and runs along the ground to his feet.

HOT TIP

You can add more than one spotlight glow if you like: simply duplicate the glow and flip it to come in from the opposite side of the image. If you do this, be sure to add an additional shadow behind the man, cast by that light.

91

Shading using Hard Light

WHEN WE LOOKED AT SHADOWS earlier in this chapter, we were always painting with dark colors. But in this scene, set in a nightclub, we want to add the impression of the singer being lit by multicolored stage lighting from different angles.

Rather than painting directly onto the girl's layer, we'll create a new layer in Hard Light mode. By painting on this, we can add the effects we want without damaging the original layer; we can also edit the effects later, to produce exactly the effect we want.

1 When we place the girl on the nightclub background, she looks quite artifically placed in the scene: her coloring in no way matches the tones of the background image. To begin, hold **ctrl** and click on the girl's thumbnail in the Layers palette to load it up as a selection. Make a new layer and, in the dialog, set the mode to Hard Light, filled with Hard Light neutral color.

4 Let's add some Lens Flare to make the scene more impressive. We could add this filter directly to the background, or to the girl – but we get far more control if we first make a new layer, filled with black. Then choose Fliter > Render > Lens Flare, and position the flare in the preview window so that it's pointing down from the left.

2 Group this new Hard Light layer with the girl's layer, so it only shows up where the two overlap. Using a soft-edged brush, sample some of the pink color from the background, and paint it on the girl's shoulder to look like light reflecting off her.

3 Continue sampling colors from the background, painting them on the Hard Light layer as appropriate. You'll need to choose fairly dark colors to paint with: too bright, and the effect will look artificial. As it's a separate layer, if we make a mistake we can easily paint over it.

Although we've used a Hard Light layer to paint in color, we could also use the technique for painting in black to create traditional shadows – or, for a more subtle look, paint them in dark brown or dark blue instead, depending on the lighting of the scene. By painting shadows on a separate layer, we keep the original intact.

5 When we change the mode of this Lens Flare layer from Normal to Screen, all the black disappears so we can see through it to the scene beneath, and move it into place.

6 In the previous step, the Lens Flare layer appeared where we created it – right at the top of the layer stack. But if we move it beneath the Hard Light layer, then it appears to originate from behind the girl's head. We can still see an outline of the ring it created in front of the girl, but the dazzling white center is hidden by the Hard Light layer.

93

Flashlight illumination

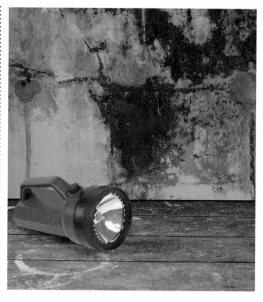

DARKNESS CAN PROVIDE AN IMAGE with a much needed change in mood; a technique frequently used in horror or thriller movies – the lurking terror is very rarely in a well lit, designer basement, after all.

Our starting image is a bit dull and lacks any sense of purpose: it's just a flashlight in a light room that may just be in the process of being renovated. Its owner's probably gone off to find his sandwich. By turning out the lights and switching on the flashlight, however, we instantly add an air of mystery to the scene: where is this place, and why has the flashlight been left lying on the ground in what appears be a derelict house? Suddenly thoughts of jolly decorators on their lunchbreak are replaced by those of deserted buldings and lurking fiends in hockey masks – or perhaps not.

1 Make sure the flashlight layer is active by clicking its thumbnail. Now make a selection around the lens. This is quite tricky because of the angle; see the sidebar for a tip on how best to achieve this. Once done press *ctrl J* twice to create two new copies.

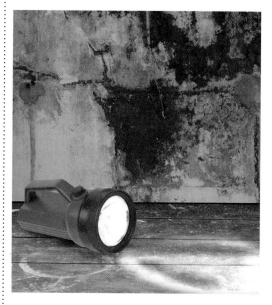

4 It's beginning to shape up but something's not right, the flashlight needs to be switched on to cast its light, of course. Make the second lens copy active and set its blend mode to Linear Dodge. This has the effect of making the already light areas much brighter.

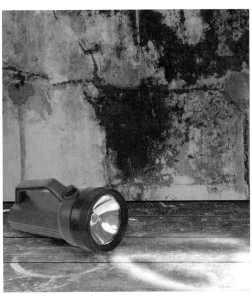

2 Press *ctrl* *T* to enter Free Transform, now stretch out one of the lens copies to create the shape of the beam area on the floor in front of the flashlight. You'll need to zoom out to see the handles as they will be outside of the canvas area. Press *Enter* to apply the transformation.

3 Press *ctrl* *I* to invert the colors of the layer. Now apply some Gaussian blur; we can use a large amount as we don't want too much of the original detail showing. Finally, set the Blend Mode to Linear Dodge. Most of it will disappear creating the effect of the beam pattern.

HOT TIP

We can't use the Elliptical Marquee to select the lens with one pass because of its odd angle. We could add several smaller selections together but that is unecessarily messy and time consuming. Instead, we can create a shape layer using the Ellipse tool, by lowering the opacity and using free transform we can easily distort it to fit the shape of the lens. We simply load its selection by pressing *alt* *Enter* and switch back to the flashlight layer to create the copies. The shape layer can be hidden for later use or deleted.

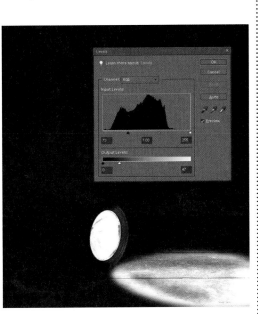

5 Load up the light beam layer's selection by holding *ctrl* and clicking its thumbnail, add the lens layer's selection by holding *Shift* *ctrl* when clicking its thumbnail. Now create a Levels adjustment layer at the top of the stack. The selection automatically creates a mask.

6 Drag the right-hand Output levels slider across to the left to lower the overall brightness. Now push the Shadows value to the right to give a richer effect. Finally, load up the flashlight's selection and use a soft black brush to paint out the mask inside the bezel to lighten it up.

95

Can I get a job doing this?

THE SHORT ANSWER IS: YES. The longer answer is: Well, yes – if you have the skill, determination and free time available, and if you happen to bump into the right people.

The question of whether it's possible to make a career out of doing photomontage work occurs, at some stage, to just about everyone who's ever dabbled in Photoshop or Elements. It's an appealing proposition: the idea of spending one's days tinkering with images for profit sounds like a great way of occupying oneself.

The trouble is, the world just isn't crying out for more photomontage artists. It's not like studying to become a dentist or a plumber. There's no standard course, no regular qualification, and absolutely no guarantee of a career of any sort at the end of the line. This, coupled with the fact that you're not alone in wanting to pursue this path, means that there are far more people out there capable of manipulating images than there is demand for such services.

But if you're really determined, then there are several steps you could take to make the dream a possibility. It all depends on whether you have the free time to develop your skills without being paid to do so.

The first, and most important step, is to get your work published. Art editors are notoriously busy and preoccupied people, who are driven by deadlines and the need to fill the space between the text and the advertisements in their publications. What matters to them are four main factors: Can you interpret a brief? Do you have the skill needed to turn in a good job? Do you have an interesting or unique style? And, above all: Can you be sure to meet a deadline? For ultimately, it doesn't matter how good or inspired your work is, if you're unable to turn it in on time. If you don't meet the deadline, you'll never hear from them again.

Art editors are far more likely to take a chance on commissioning work from an unknown artist (yourself) if you can demonstrate that others have already placed their faith in you. Of course, it's something of a Catch 22 situation: you can't get the work unless you've already had work published, and you can't get work published unless someone gives you the work.

One solution is to begin by offering your services, for free, to publications or websites who couldn't afford to pay for them. This might include local newspapers, community and sports magazines, charity websites, church and workplace newsletters, and so on. Get as much work in print or on websites as you can, to show that you're capable of sustained effort.

Only when you have a fair body of work to show should you then approach magazine and newspaper art directors. But start small: writing to *The New Yorker* offering to draw their covers is unlikely to produce a positive response, at least in the early days.

Self-promotion is a key part of bringing your skills to the attention of those who matter. These days, it's easy to set up and maintain your own website, and you should take the opportunity to show off as much published work as you can in this way. Feel free, as well, to show 'personal' work done for your own entertainment – but be aware that this won't carry as much weight with potential employers as work you've been commissioned to do.

Another way of getting started is to get a job in a publishing office, doing menial tasks such as scanning and filing photographs. Before long you'll come across an image that needs tweaking; show what you can do, and if you're any good your skills will be recognized.

You can, of course, set up a web site offering your services directly to the public. Many people offer photo restoration, custom greetings cards, and photo caricature services; a few make a reasonable living out of it.

Decide where your strengths lie. You may be proficient at restoring photographs, or removing ex-spouses from family shots, or caricaturing politicians. Develop your area of expertise, and find new ways of performing the task. People are far more likely to use you if you can offer a service that no-one else can.

CONGRATULATIONS
Fred and
Wilma
on your fortieth
wedding anniversary

■ Making cards, notices and invitations is an enjoyable hobby in Elements. But why settle for a standard, head-on view of the text when we could show it on a billboard? It's easy to distort any text or images so they appear to be viewed in perspective, giving the design far more impact.

6

Transformation and distortion

COMPOSING MULTIPLE IMAGES into a single montage almost always involves scaling, rotating and moving the elements around. In this chapter, we'll look at the basics of using that most powerful tool, Free Transform: with its multiple keyboard modifiers, it's capable of producing good results.

There's more to distortion than simply scaling and rotation, though. In this chapter we'll explore how to make an image fit a flag, a mug and a computer screen as well as several other surfaces, showing how to use Elements' tools and filters to match an image to just about any surface.

The science of transformation

W HEN PUTTING A MONTAGE TOGETHER, it's almost certain that you'll need to resize one or more of its components to fit the scene. You may also want to distort an image for a particular effect; to give it a 3D appearance such as scattering photos on a surface or placing them on a virtual gallery wall, for example.

Free Transform allows you to move, rotate, scale and distort your image in real time so you can compare and position in place to match the rest of the artwork. You can perform this on an individual layer or, if you have grouped multiple layers together, alter them in unison.

1 Press **ctrl** **T** to enter Free Transform mode. Its bounding box will appear, surrounding the layer content. The **Enter** key applies the transformation, **esc** cancels it.

2 Click and drag within the box to move the layer around the document. Placing the cursor outside the boundary and dragging will rotate the layer around the center point.

6 Hold **ctrl** while dragging a center handle to skew the image. Additionally, if the **Shift** key is also held, the skew is constrained to horizontal or vertical movement.

7 Press **ctrl** **alt** **Shift** when dragging a corner to distort the image in perspective. This can be both horizontal and vertical, depending on the direction you move the cursor.

3 By grabbing and dragging a corner handle you can scale layer up or down freely. This, by default, is relative to the opposite corner, which remains anchored in place.

4 By holding the *Shift* key whilst dragging a corner, the layer will be scaled in proportion to its original size. This option can be used when you need to ensure the shape remains constant.

5 Use the left or right center handles to adjust the width of the image. The top and bottom handles, as you might expect, scale it vertically.

HOT TIP

You'll need to be a little cautious if you intend to increase the size of the image. Too much will result in noticeable degradation, especially with photographs, as Elements has to add pixels to compensate. Wherever possible it's better to start with a larger image and reduce it to fit.

8 You can distort the image freely by holding *ctrl* when dragging a corner handle. This can be used to accurately match an existing part of the artwork: a billboard, for example.

9 Use the *alt* key to force the image to scale around the center point, rather than the opposite corner. This works with most of the transformation modes.

10 You can change the reference point to one of nine positions from the Options Toolbar. This allows you to rotate the image using a different pivotal point.

Distorted field of vision

1 Here's our field with a single sunflower. We'll start by duplicating the flower. Make sure it's the active layer. Press **ctrl J**. This is normally used to create a layer from a selection; as there isn't one defined here, it simply copies the entire image.

BY MIMICKING PHOTOGRAPHIC EFFECTS we can fool the viewer into believing an image is real, if only temporarily. This technique has been used frequently in the movies, television and other media – especially before digital technology was accessible. Indoor sets would have lavishly painted backdrops to give the impression they were shot on location. The scenery would be out of focus and not instantly recognised as fake.

We'll use this trick here to create a field of sunflowers using just a single object duplicated and scaled down many times. One larger flower is kept in the foreground drawing focus away from the rest. The copies are all partially covered by one another; this prevents the viewer making an instant comparison. By blurring the rear rows and background, we are fooled into believing they extend far into the distance; we are accustomed to seeing photographs taken with a shallow depth of field so we don't question it.

4 We can make some adjustments to the row. We'll begin by swapping some of the layers around. This gives us a more uneven appearance. To do this, click and drag the thumbnails above or below one another in the Layers palette. Keep them behind the original flower, of course.

7 Press **ctrl J** to duplicate the current layer. Select the layer behind. Scale it down quite a way. Now duplicate it. Move them both to create a long row. Press **ctrl E** to merge them. Repeat this a couple more times until the foreground is more or less hidden.

2 Click the original flower layer's thumbnail. Press **ctrl T**. Press and hold **Shift** to maintain the proportions. Click and drag the top right handle to scale the flower down. Click and drag inside the box to offset it from the original. Keep it a little lower than the foreground flower.

3 Now we'll complete the initial row. Press **alt ctrl T**. Instead of transforming the current layer, it will create a new one. Adjust the size and position as before. Add another two or three copies. Keep them evenly spaced. They wouldn't be growing too close together.

HOT TIP

If you're using a version of Elements which doesn't support layer grouping, you'll need to create the merged layers in a slightly different way: start by creating a new layer above the layers you want to merge. Link the images together by clicking the empty box to the left of their thumbnails in the Layers palette. Using the keyboard shortcut **ctrl alt E** will duplicate and stamp the layers down to the new empty one.

5 Now we'll start adding the rows behind. Group all four flower layers by multi-selecting them in the palette. Press **ctrl alt E** to stamp them onto a new layer. This will be created above the group so drag it down the stack so it sits behind the others.

6 We'll fill that empty ground space behind the front row. Flip the layer horizontally from the Image>Rotate menu. Use Free Transform to scale and position the layer so its stalks are staggered behind the front row. Because they're hidden we can distort them a little more than before.

8 To create the impression of depth we'll add some Gaussian Blur. Start with the first merged group. Add a small amount of blur; enough to knock the focus out. Move to the next adding a little more. When you've finished with the flowers you can blur the background to match.

9 The ground beneath the flowers is still visible and noticeably blurred. Grab the Burn Tool **O**. Set the mode to Highlights. Now use a large soft brush to paint in shadow over the grass. Finally, select the foremost flower rows. Add some shadow to their stems to complete the effect.

Simple perspective distortion

ONE OF THE MOST USED distortion techniques in photomontage is to add or replace an image where it will be viewed in perspective. This could be anything from a photo lying on a table to a billboard in a street scene.

As we'll discover in the following tutorial: this effect can be achieved quickly and simply using the Free Transform tool. The task is made easier still if we already have a basis for our distortion; the laptop's screen in our example. We'll also see how the effect can be made more realistic by blending the images to retain the original highlights of the screen.

1 Here we have our laptop along with the image we want placed on its screen. We'll use the screen's existing perspective as our guideline. Firstly, make sure the flower is the currently active layer by click its thumbnail in the Layers palette.

Now enter Free Transform mode by pressing *ctrl* *T*. We'll begin by moving the image roughly into position. Click and hold within the bounding box. Now drag the photo across so it's covering the laptop's screen.

3 The image is now more or less in place. Check to see if any fine tuning is needed. It's best to do this before you commit the transformation. This is mainly to avoid further quailty loss but also because subsequent editing will result in the transform tool's bounding box being squared off to the document, rather than conforming to the image as it is now; making it very awkward to align the image. Simply grab and adjust any of the point(s) as before.

2 Press and hold *ctrl*. This puts us into Distort mode allowing the individual control points to be freely manipulated. Start by clicking and dragging one of the corners to the corresponding corner of the laptop's screen. Try to leave a little space between the new image and the bezel of the laptop. This adds a bit more realism as displays generally don't extend right up to the edges. Repeat the process for the remaining three corners.

4 With the distortion applied the photo of the flower looks much more a part of the whole image. It's still not completely convincing, though. Adding the new layer has hidden the reflection and shading on the original screen. This has made the display seem a little flat. We'll fix this by changing the photo layer's blend mode; in this instance using the aptly named Screen. As the base layer is black, the two images blend allowing the highlights to appear over the photo.

Wrapping around surfaces

ADDING ARTWORK TO CURVED SURFACES can present the montage artist with all manner of problems to overcome. The most awkward being objects such as cylinders. When they are viewed at an angle the perspective effect causes not only the width to recede as it moves further from the camera but the depth of the curves become considerably different between the top and base.

In these situations, applying a uniform distortion to the artwork simply won't do the trick. The result will be confusing and look unrealistic. There is, of course, a solution; demonstrated here by placing a graphic around the surface of a plain coffee mug.

1 Although it's not obvious at this stage; as a result of the perspective effect, the slight angle at which this mug has been photographed causes the depth of the curves at the top and bottom to be different depths. This will be far more noticeable when the artwork is applied and initially distorted.

4 Open the Shear filter dialog. By default, there is no distortion. Control points can be added by clicking and dragging on the line. It's better to create these towards the edge, rather than a single point in the centre. This gives a smoother curve. You can see the effect in the preview.

5 The artwork has been rotated back to the correct orientation. As you can see, the top is true to the curve of the mug but the bottom is far too shallow. Firstly, enter Free Transform mode. Holding *ctrl*, drag the bottom corners in to match the perspective of the mug's edges.

2 The artwork has been imported from a separate file. Press **ctrl T** to enter Free Transform. Holding **alt** and **Shift**, scale the artwork down to the appropriate size. Using the modifier keys ensures it's scaled proportionately and remains centered.

3 Before we can apply the distortion, the artwork must be rotated by 90°. The Shear filter only operates on the horizontal axis. This can be achieved with Free Transform (hold **Shift** to constrain to 45° increments) or from the menu: Image > Rotate > Layer 90° Right.

6 Open up the Liquify filter (under Distort in the Filters menu). Select the Warp tool. Using a large brush, drag out the lower part of the artwork to increase the curve's depth. Try to use as few strokes as possible to avoid the edge becoming uneven.

7 Our artwork now fits the shape perfectly. It still looks a little out of place, though. The problem is that the mug has shadows and reflections whereas the artwork appears flat. This is easily solved. Set the layer's blend mode to Multiply. Finally, lower the opacity a little.

HOT TIP

The display in the Liquify dialog only shows the active layer. This makes it difficult to match up with the existing image. Before you open the filter, move the document window over to one side. You can then resize the filter's window and place it next to the original for reference.

Making curls and folds

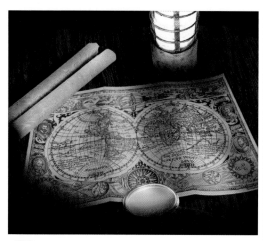

PAPER TENDS TO HOLD ITS SHAPE after being folded or rolled up for any length of time. This can be an annoyance in everyday life; as anyone who has experience of hanging wallpaper will testify. In the controllable world of digital montage, however, we can use these traits to our advantage.

In this tutorial, we'll see how distortion and shading can transform a piece of flat artwork into a convincing three-dimensional map; one that has been rolled and folded many times. Of course, the technique can be customized for many other situations.

1 We first need to add some extra blank space to accommodate the distortion. We'll do this by increasing the canvas, rather than shrinking the artwork. Press **alt** **ctrl** **C** to open the Canvas Size dialog. Check the Relative box. Increase the size by around 30%.

4 Rotate the canvas 90° right. With the Marquee tool still selected. Position the cursor in the center of the right panel. Click and hold to start a selection. Hold the **alt** key. Drag out the bounding box to the edge of the canvas. This ensures the distortion will be centered on the layer.

7 Create a new layer at the top of the stack. Hold **ctrl** and click the left panel's layer thumbnail. Now add and hold the **Shift** key. Click the other two layers in turn to add their selections. Fill this with 50% Gray. Press **ctrl** **D** to deselect. Set the layer's blend mode to Hard Light.

8 Load up the selection for one of the panels. Add some highlight and shadow using Dodge and Burn (see the chapter on Lighting for more on this technique). Because we've restricted the area, we get a nice solid crease line. Repeat for each of the other panels.

2 We need to separate the artwork into sections. We'll use the map's original fold lines as a guide. Grab the Rectangular Marquee **M**. Line the cursor up with the left fold line. Now drag out the selection to enclose that panel. Press **ctrl Shift J** to cut it to a new layer.

3 Press **alt [** to re-enable the previous layer. Now select the right panel. Again, cut this to a new layer. You'll now have 3 individual pieces. Optionally, you can press **ctrl [** to move the layer down the stack; there's no benefit other than having them in a logical order.

5 Open the Shear filter. We want our edges to be curling upwards so the bend needs to go to the left. Click on the grid to add two new control points. Drag them out to form a shallow curve. Repeat this for the other two layers; vary the curves a little on each.

6 Rotate the canvas back. Make the left panel layer active. Press **ctrl T** to enter Free Transform. Position the cursor over the right-middle handle. Hold **ctrl Shift**. Click and drag to match it up to the adjacent layer. You may also want to raise its opposite edge as well.

9 Hide the background layer by clicking its eyeball icon. Press **ctrl Shift E** to merge the visible layers. Press **ctrl T**. Hold **ctrl alt Shift**. Click and drag a top corner in towards the center. Reduce the height with the top-center handle.

10 Load up the map's selection. Hold **alt**. Use the cursor keys to nudge up by one pixel. This gives the impression that the map has thickness. All that remains is to add a shadow. This is simply a copy of the map layer flipped and distorted. Finally it's blurred and the opacity lowered.

109

The ripple effect

1 We'll begin by selecting the leaf and copying it to a new layer. The background layer has been filled with 50% gray, which will allow us to fine-tune the effect once everything is in place. We'll hide the leaf's layer for the time being whilst we create the water texture.

RESPECT WHERE IT'S DUE to the photographers with the skill and, more importantly, the patience to capture the ubiquitous image of a leaf or other such object causing delicate ripples as it lands on water. As pretty and serene as this all is, many of us simply don't have the time to wait for that perfect moment. We don't need to, of course. The effect can be recreated quickly with neither a tree or a lake to be seen.

We photographed the leaf at a suitable angle to avoid the need to make excessive changes to fit in with the rest of the scene. We'll use a few different distortion techniques here. The main effect is creating the ripples; we'll use the rather misleadingly named ZigZag filter to create this.

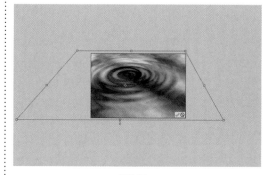

4 Enter Free Transform **ctrl T**. You'll need to zoom out (see Hot Tip). Hold **ctrl alt Shift**. Drag one of the bottom corner handles outward to alter the perspective. Release the keys. Hold **Shift**. Drag a corner point again to scale the image up to the required size.

7 The leaf looks a too flat on the surface as it has no reflection. Duplicate the layer **ctrl J**. Switch back to the original by clicking its thumbnail. Set the blend mode to Multiply. Now use free transform to distort the copy and give the leaf some depth.

2 Create a new layer. Press **D** to ensure you're using the default black and white palette. Fill the layer with the Clouds filter. We want a good spread of tones here. You can rerun the filter a few times by pressing **ctrl F** until you're happy with the result.

3 Now to make the ripples. Select the ZigZag filter from the Render sub-menu. Select Pond Ripples as the style. We're creating a close-up image so we only need a small amount of ridges but a large amount of distortion. The exact settings will vary from image to image, of course.

5 We'll add some highlights using the Plastic Wrap filter (found under the Artistic sub-menu). Keep the effect subtle: overdoing it will leave us with syrup rather than water. Apply the filter. Lastly, press **ctrl Shift L** to boost the contrast with Auto Levels.

6 With the ripples in place we can make the leaf layer visible again. Make sure it's the top most layer. Drag it to the top of the stack in the layers palette if necessary. We'll use Free Transform to alter its size and adjust the perspective slightly.

HOT TIP

It can be difficult to use free transform when the area takes up the entire size of the document, especially if you need to expand it. Press **ctrl —** a couple of times to zoom out. You'll now be able to see the whole image and have space to use the control handles. If you are not using the maximized view mode, you'll need to drag the window out as well. This can be changed in the program's preferences by unchecking Zoom Resizes Windows.

8 We'll add a sense of movement by distorting the reflection. Open the Ripple filter. Set the size to medium. Increase the amount gradually to give it a slight distortion. Soften it down by applying a small amount of Gaussian Blur. Lastly, lower the opacity a little.

9 Set the water layer's blend mode to Overlay. Switch to the Background layer. Open the Hue/Saturation dialog **ctrl U**. Check the Colorize box. Now adjust the hue and saturation to suit the image. Finally drop the water layer's opacity to soften the effect.

A flag for all nations

1 Here's our flag artwork. This is a rasterized vector image. Graphic objects such as this work really well in this format. They can be rendered at any size and will never lose their quality. Be sure to leave space around the image to allow for the distortion effects.

COMPONENTS OF A MONTAGE OR EFFECT are often created from the most unlikely of sources. The above image for instance: Just a photo of an old bedsheet hanging up? Well yes, it is, but for the resourceful and imaginative artist, it can be a whole lot more!

We'll be using the image with the Displace filter to transform a two-dimesional graphic of the Stars and Stripes into a realistic flag blowing in the breeze. The technique is versatile, too. As well as fabrics, it can be used with many other types of texture; almost anything which has a raised pattern such as rock, tiles or even the bark of a tree. In our example, the image can be saved as a template which can be reused with different nationality images or patterns.

4 The Displace filter uses a separate texture map document to apply its distortion effect. Select Duplicate Layer from the Layer menu. Choose New for the destination. You'll need to give it a name. This will create a new copy of our grayscale sheet.

7 Turn the sheet layer back on. Set its blend mode to Multiply. The effect is taking shape but there's a bit of a problem: the two layers no longer match; as yet only the flag has been distorted. Press *ctrl* *F* to reapply the filter using the same settings, without opening the dialog again.

2 The sheet image has been opened with the Place command under the File menu. Once loaded it behaves in a similar way to free transform. Here it's been rotated and resized to match the flag graphic. Pressing *Enter* accepts the changes and adds the image on a new layer.

3 Press *ctrl* *Shift* *U* to desaturate the new layer. We don't need the color, just the tones of the folds. Add some more contrast by tightening up the highlights and shadows using levels. This will give a much stonger effect when for the texture map and overlay.

5 Load the layer's selection by holding *ctrl* and clicking its thumbnail. Apply a Crop from the Image menu to remove the excess from around the image. Now apply some Gaussian Blur. We need to keep the tones but soften the harsh edges. Finally, save it in Photoshop format.

6 Go back to the flag document. Turn off the sheet layer for now and make the flag layer active. Open the Displace filter dialog. Use the default settings and click OK. A file dialog will appear. Browse to where you saved the texture map. Double-click the file to apply the filter.

There will be occasions where you find the filter has caused areas of unwanted distortion; as with some of the stars on the flag. This is largely unavoidable as the image has been stretched too far over an area of strong contrast. You can often disguise the problem with a carefully placed foreground object or perhaps, as with our final image, some blur, if the context allows. You could, of course, use the Liquify filter to reposition them, too.

8 We'll add a shallow wave to the flag. Group the two layers. Press *ctrl* *alt* *E* to create a merged copy. Hide the original layers. Now rotate the image 90° Left. Open the Shear filter. Apply a very slight S curve. Rotate the layer back to its correct angle.

9 Here's our final image. A small amount of Motion Blur has been added to give a greater sense of movement. The addition of the flagpole and background boosts the realism of the scene. Save as a Photoshop document; you can always return to the image to change the nationality.

Not so extreme close up

FILTERS OFTEN SUFFER FROM ABUSE; and consequently can quickly achieve cliché status. Even though their effects can be gradually increased, there is too much of a temptation to take it straight to the extreme. Spherize is one such casualty. Because of its potential for caricature, it rarely sees anything between -100% and 100%. It can, however, be used for much more subtle duties.

The following example uses the filter in moderation to create the illusion of an image being enlarged through a magnifying glass. In this instance on a collection of postage stamps. You'll also see how glass can be replaced using layer styles and blend modes. This is a great effect for drawing attention to something in your artwork or simply as a realistic component.

1 Here's our magnifier, with the original glass removed. Hold *ctrl* and click the New Layer icon in the Layers palette. This will create the layer beneath the magnifier. Make a selection around the inside edge of the frame with the Elliptical Marquee *M*. Fill this with 50% Gray.

4 We'll create a shadow to add depth. Create another layer. Load the magnifier frame's selection. Fill the selection with black. Now load the glass layer's selection. This time fill it with a light gray. Press *ctrl* *D* to deselect. Now apply some Gaussian Blur.

IMAGES: POSTAGE STAMPS – WIKIPEDIA COMMONS; MAGNIFYING GLASS – DAVIDE GUGLIELMO (STOCK.XCHNG.COM)

2 Select the Dodge tool and set the Mode to Highlights. Now use a large soft brush to paint in a large area of highlight. Use a low exposure, building the effect up with several strokes. Reduce the brush size and add a couple of random spot effects for good measure.

3 We'll use layer styles to give our glass some substance. Begin by applying the Scalloped Edge Bevel preset. Now add a High Inner Shadow. Set the layer's blend mode to Hard Light. The gray becomes invisible; leaving us with just our highlights and styles showing. Lower the opacity slightly.

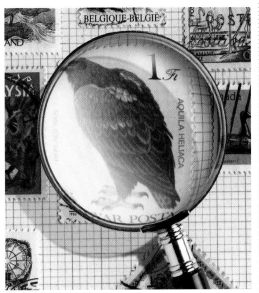

5 Press *ctrl* **T** for Free Transform. Scale, rotate and reposition the shadow layer to give the impression the magnifying glass is a distance above the background. Set the blend mode to Multiply. Finally, lower the opacity. The lighter gray fill now looks like diffusion through the glass.

6 Duplicate the background layer. Load up the glass layer's selection. Open the Spherize filter. Apply the desired amount of distortion to the copy of the background; 80% in the example. Click the Shadow layer's thumbnail to make it active. Press *ctrl* **F** to reapply the filter.

HOT TIP

Using selections to constrain filters is not only used for localizing the affected area. If you also feather the selection first, the effect of the filter will be blended in or its strength lessened as it reaches the edge of the selected area.

115

Smoke without fire

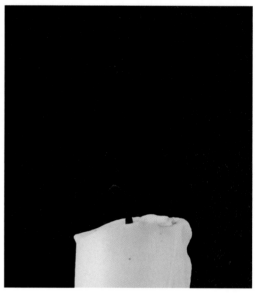

1 Here's our candle. It's been placed on a black background to make the effect easier to see whilst we're putting it together. This can always be replaced with a more fitting backdrop once it's finished. We'll begin by adding a new layer **ctrl** **alt** **Shift** **N**.

PHOTOGRAPHING SMOKE CAN BE TRICKY. You need to get the lighting correct and capture the picture at just the right moment or you'll have to start again from the beginning. Even when you do have an image you're happy with, using it in a montage involves a lot of fiddly selections and masking. Creating the effect from scratch is not as difficult as you might think.

In the following tutorial we'll see how smoke can be conjured up quickly and easily using the Liquify filter. Its range of tools lets you manipulate an image as though it were oil on water; this can produce natural looking free-form effects.

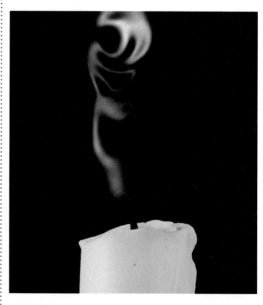

4 Add another new layer. Create a clipping group with the smoke layer **ctrl** **G**. Press **D** to restore the palette to its default. Fill the layer with the Clouds filter, which gives us a more random texture. Merge the two layers together by pressing **ctrl** **E**.

2 Select the Rectangular Marquee **M**. Draw out a long thin box from the wick to the top of the image. Fill the selection with a strong color, red in this instance; it needs to show up well in the Liquify dialog. Press **ctrl D** to deselect. Lastly add some Gaussian Blur to create a soft edge.

3 Now for the fun part. Open the Liquify filter from the Distort sub-menu. Experiment using a combination of the tools to spread and distort the line. Vary the brush size and pressure to create a more random effect. If you're using a pressure sensitive tablet, check the Stylus Pressure box.

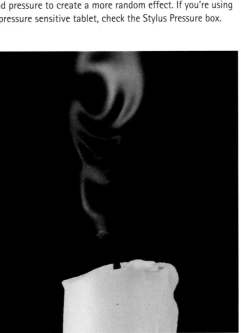

5 You can fine-tune the effect using Free Transform; hold **ctrl** to adjust the corner points independently. Here the base of the smoke has been tapered in slightly and the top widened. The opacity has also been lowered a little to make the effect a little more subtle.

6 Create a layer above the candle itself, and change its blend mode to Color Dodge. Set the foreground color to orange. Now use a soft, low opacity brush to paint in a small glow on the end of the wick. A hint of blue has been added to the smoke using a cooling Photo Filter adjustment layer.

HOT TIP

The Liquify filter can be a little hit and miss. If you make a mistake, pressing **ctrl alt Z** steps backwards progressively. You also have the ability to restore areas selectively with the Reconstruct tool **E**. Simply paint over the required area to undo the changes. Varying the brush pressure controls the speed at which the image is rebuilt. If you decide to start afresh, click the Revert button. This will return the image to its initial state without having to exit from the dialog first.

117

Drawing comparisons

ONE OF THE QUESTIONS MOST FREQUENTLY ASKED by newcomers to digital imaging is which program should they choose: Photoshop Elements or the full Photoshop product. There is no definitive answer; each has its merits. The basis for the decision should be one of individual requirements.

A common misconception is that Elements is Photoshop's poor relation, only suitable for photography hobbyists who need a simple program to catalog their images and perform quick fixes such as removing red-eye from portraits or correcting color casts. Although there is a definite leaning toward the amateur market, it is more than capable of producing the same standard of artwork as its big brother. Elements still has around 90% of the features found in Photoshop; it merely lacks some of the more high end functionality associated with professional pre-press. You'll find all the same filters and the majority of adjustments are present. Some are cut-down versions offering less in the way of fine tuning, though not at the expense of their usefulness. There is also a degree of symbiosis between the two programs. Look under the hood of Elements and you'll find technologies from recent Photoshop releases packaged to perform a specific purpose. Similarly there are parts of Elements that have traversed the other way.

There is, of course, one distinct difference: the price. Presently, Photoshop will happily relieve your bank account of $600 upwards, depending on the version you choose. Elements, on the other hand, will cost you around $100 for the full product (less for an upgrade from previous versions). This makes it an ideal solution if you have a limited budget.

So, with all that said, what exactly are the differences between the two programs and can you survive without whatever it is that's missing? As we mentioned before, Elements does not feature some of the tools required for press quality printing such as comprehensive color management and the CMYK color space. This, however, does not mean it cannot be used professionally; the images in this book were all produced using it, after all. Most designers' applications such as Adobe's InDesign will convert the images and to an extent, allow you to adjust the color. There are also many 3rd party utilities which perform the same function; Apple's OS X has Graphic Converter, for example.

The differences become less of an issue when you start comparing the tools and commands. Many of Elements' shortfalls can be overcome with a little lateral thinking. Here are the main 'extras' found in Photoshop, with workarounds:

Photoshop tool	What it does	Elements workaround
Pen tool	Draws Bézier paths	Use selections instead, and save as Alpha channels; save as .psd or JPEG2000 file
Curves adjustment	Adjusts color and brightness	Use Levels instead
Vanishing Point filter	Places images in scene in perspective	Use Free Transform to distort layer
Black & White adjustment	Changes color image to monochrome	Use Gradient Map adjustment layer with default colors
Layer masks	Allow user to hide image areas	Use Adjustment Layer (see p40) or import Photoshop layer mask (see p41)
Layer styles	More control over layer styles	Be creative with built-in styles, or import styles from Photoshop
CMYK mode	Prepares artwork for commercial printing	Use third party software to convert to CMYK mode
Smart Filters	Allows editable filters with selective masking	Duplicate target layer, and lower opacity, use Adjustment layer mask to hide effect
Image Warp	Allows free distortion of layers	Use Shear or Liquify filters for similar effect

There are some features in the full Photoshop that have no Elements equivalent – such as Smart Objects, Video and 3D Layers (Photoshop Extended edition only) and support for specialist video modes. But in the main, Elements is capable of satisfying 99% of every montage artist and photographer's requirements.

■ Textures can make all the difference to a piece of artwork. Here are two versions of a wedding album layout. The first is flat and uninspiring, everything is clean and squared off. The second with its satin background and gold framed images sets the mood and adds that all important interest factor.

7

Materials and textures

OUR SURROUNDINGS ARE DEFINED BY TEXTURES. We can, for example, see at a glance that something is made of wood simply because of its familiar grainy appearance. We recognize certain materials such as silk by the way the light catches its folds and creases.

In this chapter, we'll look at ways of creating textures such as wood and cloth from scratch. This gives you more freedom as you are not constrained to the size of your source images.

We'll also see how existing images can be manipulated to match your theme: torn edges for newspaper clippings or ticket stubs, or ageing an object by covering it in dust.

Curtains with a difference

A LL THE WORLD'S A STAGE, as William Shakespeare would have us believe; and what stage would be complete without the familiar heavy red and gold drape curtains?

The following tutorial demonstrates a quick and easy way of creating an undulating texture resembling the folds of heavy hanging material. This has many potential uses: you may want to mock up some decor for a room in the house. You could also use the effect to create a template or intro for a home movie DVD; or as with our completed image, give a family member the stardom they deserve.

1 Start with a blank document. Create a new layer, and select the Gradient Tool **G**. Choose a Linear black, white gradient. From the Options toolbar. Set the blend mode to Difference. Now position the cursor at the left edge. Hold **Shift**. Click and drag a short distance to the right.

4 Next we'll be adding some texture. Create a new layer. Use the Rectangular Marquee **M** to draw a selection that encloses nearly all of the image. Leave a narrow rectangular section across the bottom of the document. Fill the selection with 50% gray.

7 The effect is now looking much better but is still a little two dimensional. Deselect then press **ctrl T** to enter Free Transform. Click the bottom center handle. Drag it up a little way to create a small gap at the bottom of the image. This gives us some space for adjustment.

2 Reposition the cursor back to the left; around half the previous width works well. Now click and drag to the right again (remember to hold **Shift**). Repeat the process across the entire document. Vary the distance slightly each time to create the random pleats.

3 It's starting to take shape but the lines are a little strong at the moment; making the effect look too rigid. We'll soften the image with a little Gaussian Blur. Add just enough to smooth out the harsh edges giving the impression of soft, rolling fabric.

HOT TIP

At first glance, the Liquify filter often appears to be cumbersome and only useful when creating over the top effects such as caricatures or surreal Dali style images. When used conservatively and with a little patience, you can use it to manipulate smaller areas of an image to add subtle alterations to fit into a scene more convincingly.

5 Open the Fibers filter. Use low Variance and Strength settings to create an even, low contrast pattern. Set the layer's Blend Mode to Multiply. This mixes the two layers, darkening the tones at the same time. Finally, lower the opacity so the texture is visible but not too harsh.

6 Press **ctrl E** to merge the two layers. Open the Hue/Saturation dialog **ctrl U**. Check the colorize box. Now use the sliders to create a deep red color. Inverse the selection with **ctrl Shift I**. Open Hue/Saturation again. This time, create a golden yellow.

8 Open up the Liquify filter. Select the Warp tool. Choose a fairly large brush. Zoom in on the base of the curtain. Now use the brush to distort the tops and bottoms of the gold trim. As viewers. we're most likely to be above this line, so perspective determines the curves will face downwards.

9 Our curtain effect is complete. All that remains is to add a cutout from the photo of Auntie Mabel singing the Broadway hits on her birthday. Techniques for adding the spotlight and shadow can be found in Chapter 5, Light and Shade.

Quick and easy wood grain

1 Open a new document. Create a layer **ctrl** **alt** **Shift** **N**. Use the Rectangular Marquee **M** to draw a suitably sized selection. Fill this with 50% Gray. Duplicate the layer **ctrl** **J**. Bring the selection back by holding **ctrl** and clicking either layer's thumbnail.

PHOTOS OF WOOD TEXTURES can be found in almost any stock library. You can, of course, take your own. As abundant as they may be, sometimes you may not be able to find just the right style to use in your artwork. Here's where filters come to the rescue.

On the previous page, we saw how the Fibers filter can be used to create the effect of plush material. Here, we'll use it to generate the effect of wood grain – it's very versatile. To further the realism, various inconsistencies such as knots and twists are added. Just like the real thing; once made, you can use it to apply to all sorts of objects: an ornate picture frame (as the inset shows), some polished flooring, or simply as a backdrop for your images.

4 Add a few more knots and distortions; experiment with the different tools like Bloat and Twirl. When you're happy with the effect, click OK. Set the Layer's Blend Mode to Overlay. Although you won't notice any difference just yet, we're setting the layer up to allow color to be added.

2 Make sure the foreground and background colors are set to the default black and white by pressing **D**. Open the Fibers filter dialog. Adjust the settings until you have a fairly reasonable looking grain. Variance gives more randomness; Strength gives more contrast to the effect.

3 We'll add some variations such as knot holes. Open the Liquify filter. Grab the Turbulence tool. Set a medium brush. Increase the pressure a little. Position the cursor in a suitable area. Click and drag a short distance down. If it doesn't work the first time, hit **ctrl Z** and try again.

HOT TIP

A lot of the techniques in this book make use of neutral gray layers for shading and applying filters which can be controlled with blend modes. A time saving tip is to try and keep the Fill dialog set to 50% Gray. By doing this you can then use the keyboard shortcuts *Shift* Backspace and then *Enter* to quickly fill the layer or selection.

5 Click the plain gray layer's thumbnail to make it active. Open up the Hue/Saturation dialog **ctrl U**. Check the Colorize box. You'll see the effect immediately. Use the hue, saturation and lightness sliders to create the shade you want your wood to be.

6 You may decide the grain layer is too dark or coarse. Try experimenting with different blend modes. You could also use the Levels dialog to change the contrast, making it lighter or darker. Here, we've changed the blend mode to Soft Light and lowered the opacity a little.

125

Lying on a bed of satin

CREATING COMPLEX TEXTURES from scratch is not necessarily as difficult as it may at first seem. Earlier in the chapter we used gradients to create the folds of heavy curtains. A similar method can be employed to produce a more random and fluid effect resembling the intricate folds and wrinkles of finer fabrics. The major advantage of generating your own materials in this way is you are never tied to the size of a stock image. You can create the pattern to suit the dimensions of your artwork; without fear of repetition letting the effect down.

1 Hide the rose layer. Click the backgound layer's thumbnail to make it active. Select the Gradient tool G. Choose a linear black, white gradient. Set the mode to Difference; then click and drag the guide from corner to corner. This creates a good base for the effect.

4 Go to the Stylize filters submenu and select Find Edges. This produces a smoother version of our pattern and leaves the ridges well defined. It's looking good so far but we need to bring back some of the contrast. This is easily done by applying Auto Levels ctrl Shift L.

2 Pick a random starting point. Click and drag out another gradient. Make it shorter than before, and repeat this several times. Change the position, length and angle on each. Try to create a good balance of small, intricate areas and larger smooth sections.

3 The initial result is a little harsh, so we'll soften it with a little Gaussian Blur. Set a fairly low value; enough to remove the sharpness from the lines and produce a smooth transition between the tones. The amount will, of course, vary depending on the size of the document.

5 Open up the Diffuse Glow filter from the Distort sub-menu. We'll use this to add some texture and spread out the highlights. Push the Graininess up: around half way is sufficient. Add a small amount of Glow; be careful not to wash the image out. Set the clear amount to its maximum.

6 As a final step we'll add some color. The Hue/Saturation adjustment is perfect for this. Remember to check the colorize box. Some shading has been added to the rose along with a shadow to gel the scene together. More on this can be found in the Lighting chapter.

127

Making notepaper

USING PAPER IN A DESIGN can add that all-important handmade feel to it. This might be a piece of rich parchment declaring a special occasion or just a simple Post—It note to draw attention to a particular area of the artwork.

In this tutorial we'll create a piece of ruled notepaper using layers and selections. A key point to consider when creating objects from scratch is to give them some texture; in this case by adding some Gaussian noise. This helps them to blend into a montage more convincingly – real life is never as pure as a digitally produced image.

1 Start by creating a new layer. Use the rectangular marquee to mark out the shape of your paper. Fill this with white. You can't see any difference, of course, as it is displaying against white. You can either hide the backround layer or fill it to make it easier to work on the image.

4 We need to remove the excess part of the box. Hold *ctrl*. Click the paper layer's thumbnail to load its selection. Inverse the selection *ctrl* *Shift* *I*. Now remove the unwanted area by pressing *Delete*. This leaves us with a single line trimmed to fit.

5 Load the line's selection. Select the Move tool *V*. Press and hold *alt* *Shift*. Tap the down arrow key once. This duplicates the line. Hold *Shift* on its own. Nudge the line down a couple more times to create the spacing. Now repeat the process to fill the page.

2 Lock the paper layer's pixels with the icon in the layer palette or by pressing ⊘. This prevents the transparent areas from being affected. Select Add Noise from the Filter menu. Check the Monochromatic and Gaussian options. You don't need much, just enough to give a little texture.

3 Create another new layer. Draw a new rectangular selection positioning the bottom edge where the first line on the page will be. The rest of the box needs to extend outside the area of the paper. Select Stroke from the Edit menu. Set the width and color for the desired effect.

HOT TIP

Creating a selection before using the Move tool to duplicate parts of your artwork results in the copied area staying on the same layer. This is particularly useful when creating repeating patterns as we have here. Without doing so, we would end up with too many unnecessary layers.

6 Create the vertical margin using the same method as the horizontal line. I've chosen a different color here. By lowering the opacity we can control the faintness of the lines. When you're happy with the result press *ctrl E* to merge the ruled layer with the page.

7 To create the punched holes: draw a small circle using the Elliptical marquee. Press *Backspace* to clear the pixels. Click and hold inside the selection. Hold *Shift* to constrain the movement. Drag the selection down into position. Delete the pixels again.

The art of paper tearing

COMPONENTS OF YOUR ARTWORK often need a more hand-made appearance, rather than the clean, precise lines of a selection or crop. Images such as the newspaper clipping above look far more realistic with a roughly torn edge.

As you'll see in the following work through, it only takes a few quick steps to achieve the desired effect. The technique is also highly versatile and is easily adapted to a suit a variety of styles. You might, for example, want to create an old treasure map or a background of notepaper for a web page.

1 We'll use a scan of some crumpled paper. It's been placed on a separate layer. It's a good idea to work on a plain, contrasting background. This makes it easier to see what you're doing. Begin by loading up the paper layer's selection by holding *ctrl* and clicking its thumbnail.

4 Click the New Effect Layer icon at the bottom of the dialog. This creates another instance of the current filter. Use the menu to select Torn Edges. This adds a little more refinement. Again, use the sliders to fine tune the effect. Click OK to apply.

2 We'll be using the masking technique described in Chapter 3 to create the effect. Add a Solid Color adjustment layer beneath the artwork. The mask's shape is automatically defined from the selection. Switch to the paper layer. Press *ctrl* *G* to create a clipping group.

3 Click the adjustment layer mask icon. Select the Spatter filter from the Brush Strokes sub-menu. Create the desired effect using the sliders. The filter won't affect the rest of the image as the edge is the only area of contrast. Don't apply the filter yet.

5 You'll notice part of the effect has been lost. There are also stray black pixels. This is because the affected area falls outside of the paper layer's bounds. This is easily remedied. Press *ctrl* *T* to enter Free Transform. Use the handles to scale the mask toward the center.

6 For extra realism use a hard edged brush to erase random areas around the edge of the mask before applying the filters. You'll also need to merge the layers before you can add the image into your artwork. Turn off the background layer. Press *ctrl* *Shift* *E*.

Creating old paper

S O FAR WE'VE SEEN HOW TO MAKE crisp notepad paper and produce the appearance of fairly carefully torn edges. We're going to turn the clock back a little farther now and create the effect of old battererd parchment.

This simple yet very effective technique is quick to use and can easily be incorporated into your artwork. It is, of course, particularly useful for making old maps – as with the above image, medieval style letters and anything else that needs to appear to have withstood the ravages of time.

1 Begin by creating a new layer. Use the Freehand Lasso to draw a rough, ragged outline to mark out the edge of the paper. Apply a small amount of Feather to the selection; 1 pixel should be OK. Press **Shift** ⬅ to open the Fill dialog, select Color as the content and choose a light sandy color.

4 We have our mottled effect but it still looks too clean. We need to give it an earthier appearance: open the Film Grain filter located under the Artistic menu. use very low settings to create a subtle gritty effect across the surface of the paper.

HOT TIP

In step 3 we took the unusual action of creating a clipping group before merging the layers together. If we hadn't, it would have resulted in a thin dark edge appearing around our paper; this is due to combining layers which have been feathered. This can, of course, work in our favour if we wanted to have a slightly heavier border.

Once finished you can add artwork such as maps or line-art using the multiply blend mode. These can then be grouped so the missing areas are hidden on the image overlay as well.

2 Press **ctrl J** to duplicate the layer. Choose the Difference Clouds filter from the Render sub-menu; although we haven't constrained the effect, it only affects the area of the previous layer's pixels. The colors look a little strange this is only temporary.

3 Set the layer's blend mode to Soft Light, this gives us a nice spread of tones. Depending on the effect you require, you can lower the opacity to make it less harsh. When you're happy with the result, press **ctrl G** to group the layers, then **ctrl E** to merge them.

5 To complete the effect we'll add some dark patches around the edge: select the Burn tool **O**, set its mode to Midtones, now paint over random areas all around the perimeter. This gives the effect of the paper having been handled and battered over time.

6 As an optional step you can create some holes in the paper to enhance the effect even more. Use the Magic Wand **W** to select the darker patches of the paper, feather the selection then hit **⌫** to delete the areas. You can also darken the edges as in the last step.

Ageing a photo in minutes

THERE ARE MANY WAYS to restore old, damaged photographs. You'll find one in almost every digital imaging how-to book. In this tutorial however, we're going to do the exact opposite. By taking a perfectly good picture and applying a variety of effects we'll create the impression that it has been less than well cared for. We'll also add the appearance of it being torn.

Although this might seem a little perverse, it serves as an extreme example of what can be achieved by combining and blending existing textures with a photo. In this case, we'll use the reverse side of an old, battered book cover. The dents, folds and creases provide an excellent basis for the effect.

1 Here's our scanned book cover. It's already been scaled to match the photo. We'll start by duplicating the layer by pressing *ctrl* *J*. Hide the top copy for now by clicking its eyeball icon in the layers palette.

2 Our photo is placed on its own layer between the two covers. This is converted to a clipping group by pressing *ctrl* *G*. This hides the pixels that fall outside the cover layer giving us a nice rough edge.

6 To create the border: Click the photo layer's thumbnail to make it active. Hold *ctrl* and click one of the texture layer's thumbnails. Contract the selection; 15 pixels works well here. Inverse the selection *ctrl* *Shift* *I*. Press *Backspace*.

7 Hide the background layer. Press *ctrl* *Shift* *E* to flatten the layers. Load the layer's selection. Select the Freehand Lasso. Hold *alt* *Shift*. Draw a rough selection to isolate a corner of the image. Expand this by around 3 pixels.

8 Use the technique from the previous page to create a torn edge. Because we made the selection, it will only apply to the corner. Stop whilst you still have the mask enabled. You can see the problem. We only want the inside edge affected.

3 The sepia tone is created by adding a colorizing Hue/Saturation adjustment layer to the clipping group above the photo. The photo layer's blend mode is set to Hard Light allowing the texture to show through.

4 Select and show the top cover layer. Press *ctrl* *Shift* *U* to desaturate the image. Set its blend mode to Hard Light. Combined with the base layer this really enhances the texture.

5 The effect is a little washed out. Press *ctrl* *L* to open the Levels dialog. Start to drag the Shadows slider (left-hand triangle) across to the right to increase the contrast.

9 Load up the photo layer's selection. Inverse it. Press *Backspace* to remove the excess from the outside edges. Press *ctrl* *D* to deselect. Exit the mask view by clicking the photo layer. This time, we're not use it as a clipping mask.

10 Hold *ctrl* and click the mask's thumbnail. Press *ctrl* *Shift* *J*. This cuts away the corner to its own layer. Hide or delete the adjustment layer. Use free transform to move and rotate it away from the rest of the photo.

11 Load the corner layer's selection. Nudge it to the left by a couple of pixels. Open the fill dialog. Select color and choose a suitable background color. Set the mode to Behind. This will give a little thickness to the edge.

A quick repair job

WHILST WE'RE ON THE SUBJECT of damaged photos, it appears that this seaside Polaroid has seen better days. We could spend hours retouching and seamlessly blending the image to a state where nobody would ever know it had been in two parts. We're not going to, though. Instead, after crudely placing the the pieces together, we'll create some strips of old, worn Scotch tape to make it look as good as new, almost.

This is a slightly over the top example to illustrate the technique. You could, of course, use the effect in your scrapbook projects or to stick virtual photos up in your web gallery. With a bit of customizing, it could easily become solid electrical tape or even sticking-plasters.

1 We'll begin by putting the two halves together. They're on separate layers so we can use Free Transform to place them together. If it were a single layer, you could use the Lasso tools to select the pieces first. We want it to look botched so you'll want to leave some overlapping areas.

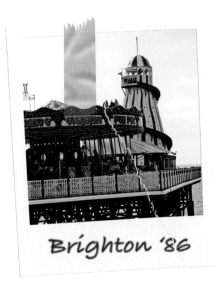

4 Select either the Dodge or Burn tool. Choose a soft brush set to Highlights. Create some light and dark shading to give the appearance of the tape lifting. You can switch between Dodge and Burn modes by holding *alt* whilst painting. Keep the effect subtle for the best results.

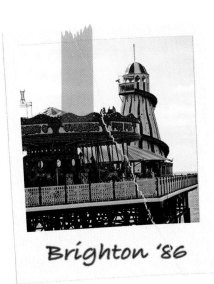

2 Create a new layer above the photo. Grab the Lasso tool **L**. Start by drawing a jagged selection. Press **alt** and release the mouse. You're now in Polygonal mode. Drag out a side. Click and hold to switch back to freehand. Add the other ragged end. Finally join it up with another straight line.

3 Press **Shift Backspace** to open the fill dialog. Select 50% gray as the Content. The hue of a neutral color can always be altered. Scotch tape is semi-opaque (even when aged) so Set the Opacity to 50%. Finally, press **ctrl D** to deselect.

If you're using a mouse to add shading it's always best to use a low opacity (or Exposure with Dodge and Burn) and build up the effect gradually. Using a pressure sensitive tablet is, of course, the best way to get the most control over the painting tools.

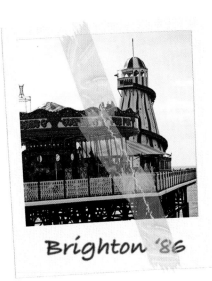

5 To give our tape a really authentic appearance we've used the Plastic Wrap filter (from the Artistic sub-menu). This is supposed to be old tape: we need to add some discoloration. A Hue/Saturation adjustment is good. You can control the effect from one dialog.

6 Press **ctrl T**. Reposition the tape. Rotate it to follow the tear. You could draw additional pieces from scratch. A quicker way is to press **alt ctrl T**. This creates a new copy on the same layer. You can flip and distort them enough to appear sufficiently different.

Letting the dust settle

DUST IS USUALLY SOMETHING we don't like seeing. As with many things, there are exceptions; wine being one. Cellars often have bottles which have rested undisturbed for many years as they reach maturity; which as a result, have accumulated a thick layer of dust.

If, however, you're not a connoisseur and need a picture in a hurry, you can create the desired effect in a few easy steps. We'll be using a bottle for the walkthrough but the technique could just as easily be applied to many different subjects: items in an attic, perhaps. You could even use it in promotional material for a cleaning company – a before and after shot, for example.

1 Here's our bottle. It's been isolated and placed on its own layer. Begin by grabbing the Selection Brush **A**. Set the Mode to Mask. Now use a soft tip to paint in the areas where you want the dust to be. Don't worry too much about spilling over the edges; they'll be tidied up.

4 Create a new layer above the bottle. Open the Fill dialog (*Shift* *Backspace*). Set the contents to 50% Gray. Choose Dissolve for the Blend Mode. Now lower the opacity a little; in this case, 75%. Dissolve uses the opacity value to determine the visibility of the layer's pixels.

2 Switch back to Selection mode. Press **ctrl** **Shift** **I** to inverse the selected areas. Hold **ctrl** **alt** **Shift**. Click the bottle layer's thumbnail. The keypress forced the selection to intersect mode. Anything outside of the bottle's edge is discarded.

3 Even a thin layer of dust has depth. We need to create some extra space for the effect to sit outside of the bottle's edge. Choose Modify > Expand from the Select menu. I've used a value of 1 pixel here. You could, of course, use different values to produce thicker layers.

HOT TIP

For extra realism, you may want to create some areas where the dust has been disturbed. This can be achieved by using a soft Eraser set to a low opacity. Parts of the layer can be progressively thinned out; great for creating fingermarks where the object has been handled.

5 The result is not too bad; it's a little uniform, though. Press **ctrl** **D** to deselect. Add some Noise to give a more random texture. Follow this with a very small amount of Gaussian Blur; you just need to take the harshness away from the effect.

6 Almost done. Select the Burn tool **O**. Set the Range to Highlights. Using the edge of a large, soft brush, darken down the sides of the dust layer. Use the shape of the bottle as a guide. Now hold **alt** to temporarily switch to Dodge mode. Lighten up the front area a little.

A little light relief

1 Here's our basic black and white artwork. Grab the Magic Wand. Uncheck the Contiguous option. This tells the tool to select every instance of the color in the image. Click anywhere in the black area. Now press *ctrl* *C* to copy the selection to the clipboard.

PREVIOUSLY, WE'VE SEEN how shading can create the illusion of depth and form; changing a simple flat object into a three-dimensional one. The same is true for creating raised surfaces. It would, of course, take far too long to paint even the most basic of textures by hand. Forutnately, Elements has a built in feature which does just that.

In this example, we'll create a traditional wax seal using a black and white logo as the basis for the effect. The edge of the artwork has been created purposely uneven to enhance the effect; giving the appearance of the hot wax spreading as the template stamp is pressed into it.

4 Press *ctrl* *V* to paste the previously saved selection then deselect. Press *ctrl* *alt* *F* to open up the Gaussian Blur dialog again. This time, set a much lower value. We need to soften the edges but keep the detail visible.

7 Open the Lighting Effects dialog. Load the saved selection from the Texture Channel menu. The effect will appear in the preview window. We've chosen to use a centered omni light here. The exact settings will vary depending on the required outcome.

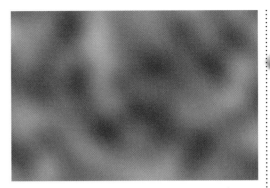

2 Press *ctrl* *D* to deselect. Add a Levels Adjustment Layer. Accept the default settings. Hold *alt* and click the mask thumbnail. Press *D* to restore the default colors. Now apply the Clouds filter. The reason for using the mask will become evident later.

3 The default effect is much too harsh for our needs. Soften it down with Gaussian Blur set to a high value. You're looking to achieve a smooth tonal blend similar to the above image. Press *ctrl* *D* when you're happy with the result.

5 Hold *ctrl* and click the mask's thumbnail to load up the selection. Only a few small areas will appear, this is OK. The boundary only shows on areas that have more than 50% opacity. Choose Save Selection from the Select menu. Give it a name and click OK.

6 Click the background layer's thumbnail. Re-enable the Magic Wand's Contiguous option. Select the area outside of the graphic. Press *ctrl* *Shift* *I* to inverse the selection. Now press *ctrl* *alt* *Shift* *N* to create a new layer. Fill with white.

8 The result is good but a little matt. Sealing wax has a mixture of flat areas and shiny highlights. The Plastic Wrap Filter is perfect for this. It can be found under the Artistic section of the Filter menu. Use the sliders to bring out the detail and give it a more moulded appearance.

9 Finally, use *ctrl* *U* to open the Hue/Saturation adjustment dialog. Click the Colorize box. Now adjust the sliders to add some color. We decided on the archetypal deep red. The image can now be saved or dragged into another piece of artwork.

Finger friendly stained glass

1 Begin by creating a new layer. Set the foreground to mid—gray. Use a small, hard tipped brush to trace the outline of the bird. It needn't be perfect as long as you capture the shape.

2 Select the entire document by pressing *ctrl* *A*. Choose Stroke Selection from the Edit menu. Set the same color and width as the brush. Use Inside as the location.

STAINED GLASS HAS BEEN AN ARTFORM for centuries. From the huge ornate windows of churches and cathedrals to the understated adornment of an urban door; people love its radiance and color.

You may have discovered the Stained Glass filter in Elements; its results are passable but tend to resemble a mosaic more than the traditional effect. In this tutorial, we'll go back to basics and create some of our effect by hand. Using a photo as a template for tracing the outline, then applying filters and layer styles to achieve our result.

This technique can be used for all kinds of project. On its own it's a great effect for greetings cards. It could also be used as an ornate border for framing a photo. You could, of course, use this technique as a basis for designing the real thing.

6 Reselect the outline layer by clicking its thumbnail. Grab the Magic Wand *W*. Click an area of the bird to select that section. The top of the head is a good place to start.

7 We need to ensure there will be no gaps between the leading and the glass. Expand the selection (Select > Modify). A value half the width of the leading is fine.

11 Open the Glass filter (under Distort). Set the texture to Frosted. A smoothness value of around 2 to 3 gives a good stipple effect. Raise the distortion level to blur the texture.

12 Change the layer's blend mode to Multiply. This filters out the lighter areas of the glass allowing the color to show through but still retains the effect.

3 The background needs to be divided up into panels. Draw a few lines between the border and the bird's outline. Use some of the contrasting areas of detail as a guide.

4 Now divide up the bird itself. Again, use the prominent details to make up the panels. Remember that each section must be completely enclosed and connected by the leading.

5 We need a separate layer for the individual colors. Press and hold *ctrl*. Click the New Layer icon in the Layer Palette. This creates a new layer beneath the curent one.

HOT TIP

As well as the four presets, you can also load custom textures into the glass filter to use as a basis for its distortion effect. Click the fly-out menu to the right of the textures menu to access the file dialog. You can use any image saved in Photoshop (psd) format.

8 Click the layer you created in step 5. Open the Fill dialog *Shift Backspace*. Set the contents to color. Use the eye-dropper to pick a suitable shade from the photo.

9 Press *ctrl D* to deselect. Color the rest of the panels by repeating the process from step 6 onwards. I've also painted the center of the eye with a small black brush.

10 Add a new layer between the color and the outline. Press *D* to restore the default foreground and background colors. Fill the layer with the Clouds filter.

13 Make the outline layer active. Select the Wow Chrome layer styles set from the Artwork and Effects palette. Apply the Beveled Edge setting. It may look a little odd at this stage.

14 Double-click the style icon to the right of the layer's thumbnail. Lower the drop shadow's distance. Adjust the bevel size. Around 6 pixels works for this size of image.

15 Here's our completed image. Adjusting the layer style has made all the difference. You may want to make the glass layer a little lighter using Levels or Brightness/Contrast.

143

Blueprint for design

1 Begin by opening the Brightness/Contrast adjustment. Drag both sliders all the way to the right to set both brightness and contrast at their maximum values. This will make the rules fainter, but won't get rid of them altogether (unless your rules are gray, rather than black).

KIDS HAVE WONDERFUL IMAGINATIONS and can come up with all kinds of fantastic inventions – such as this idea for a failsafe alarm clock involving boiling water, melting ice cubes and a tipping glass at the end of the process.

The trouble is, these designs are always sketched on whatever materials come to hand – in this case, a page torn from a spiral bound notebook. We're going to see how to turn this sketch into an official-looking blueprint: but first, we need to find a way to get rid of the lines in the background of this ruled paper.

4 Now for the blue background. If the original artwork is still your background layer, double-click its thumbnail to turn it into a regular layer; then set the mode of this layer to Screen. You won't see any difference until you make a new layer behind it, filled with blue.

2 Now desaturate the image, using **ctrl** **Shift** **U**. This will knock out all the extra colors that crept in during the previous step. Now use the Threshold adjustment to turn it to pure black and white. You may need to erase a few stray pieces of line by hand; paint them out with a white brush.

3 With the image fully cleaned up, we're ready to start turning it into a blueprint. Choose Invert to turn the image from black on white to white on black. If any of the ruled lines still show up, paint over them in black to hide them.

5 The white of the original layer is a little stark, so let's give it a touch of blue. Open the Hue/Saturation dialog, and press Colorize. Reduce the Lightness slightly, and change the Hue slider to get a pale blue; you may want to increase the Saturation a little as well.

6 Finally, let's place a graph paper grid behind the image. This grid is white on black, and we've set the opacity to just 20% to make a faint background. It's a bit of a fiddle to draw graph paper from scratch, so we've provided this for you on the CD.

HOT TIP

The hardest part of this job is cleaning up the original drawing. It would be better, of course, if kids could be persuaded to use clean, unlined paper – but when inspiration strikes, we use whatever's to hand. This is an extreme example, with solid, dark rules; most clean–up processes won't be as complex as this one. But the combination of Brightness/ Contrast and the Threshold adjustment usually does the trick.

Finding images for free

MOST OF THE TIME, you'll be using your own images for the project you're working on - you won't find a more inexpensive source than that. There will be situations, however, when you'll need a photo of an object you don't have the time or resources to take. It may be completely impractical because it's not something you normally find in your home town or even the country you live in; a famous building or indigenous animal, for example. Whilst you could improvise by altering the project or modifying an image of something similar, there is a much better way of tracking down that elusive picture: the World Wide Web.

In recent years, as more people have switched to digital cameras and fast internet connections become more commonplace, huge online stock photography sites have sprung up, containing hundreds of thousands of images. Sites such as **stock.xchng** (www.sxc.hu) and the curiously named **Morguefile.com** (traditionally a publishing term given to reference libraries of old images and cuttings) provide categorized and searchable libraries of people, places and objects from all around the world. Because they are submitted by the public for the public, the quality is not always superb; it does mean you have a good chance of finding something bizarre which would not make it past the strict scrutiny of the commercial libraries. The biggest benefit, of course, is they are completely free. The sites are kept running solely on advertising and the good will of public donations. This, of course, is great news for the montage artist on a tight or nonexistent budget.

The exact terms of use vary from site to site. Most, however, allow unlimited use for both private and commercial projects; providing it's not detrimental to either the photographer, their subject or the site itself. When you download an image, it's usually anonymously; the photographer may like to know how their photo has been used but it's rarely mandatory. Stock.Xchng allow the contributors to set their own requirements: some require you to apply for explicit permission, depending on the content - generally, and understandably, when there are recognizable faces. It's one thing to allow a someone to post photos of you but quite another to find yourself placed in an image of questionable content.

In addition to the dedicated libraries, there are also community sites such as **Flickr.com** and more recently, **Wikipedia Commons** (commons.wikipedia.org). These operate under the new Creative Commons license - a system devised for intellectual rights management on the internet. Under this license, photographers can determine what can and can't be done with their images. This ranges from complete free rein, to total copyright protection; the latter is very often negotiable through polite communication with the person concerned.

It's also worth noting the governemental public domain libraries. These offer more specific images: military, political figures and of course, there is **NASA.gov** which holds a wealth of scientific, aeronautical and astronomical photos. Again, these images are all free to use for private projects, commercial use carries some regulations; this can be found in the site's terms and conditions.

If all else fails, you can always try a search through **Google** or **Yahoo**. Both have offshoots of the site devoted to images. Great care must be taken here. Grabbing images from web searches puts you right in the middle of the copyright minefield. If you're using the pictures at a purely personal level, making backgrounds for your computer desktop and so on, you'll be OK – surveillance techniques haven't infringed the home, just yet. If, however, you intend to publish these images as part of your website or as a printed design, make sure you obtain permission from the owner of the site or photo. There's usually an address to write to. If you are in any doubt as to the copyright status, don't risk it; at the very least, you'll receive an irate email asking for removal of the image, at worst, you may find yourself in court.

As long as you respect the rules and guidelines, there is a wealth of useful content to be found. It can also be a good source of inspiration; you never know what you may come across whilst performing a search. It can often spark a whole new project idea.

A list of free sites along with links to their web addresses can be found on the book's accompanying website: **www.howtocheatinphotoshopelements.com**.

■ The text above fits neatly enough onto its plaque, but it looks rather painted on. How much more impressive if the wording appears to have been carved into the wood. The words 'First Class' in this example use a metal style not detailed in this chapter: but it's on the CD, for you to import into Elements and use in your own work.

8 Working with text

WE USE TEXT FREQUENTLY IN ELEMENTS. Although you may not think of it as being an essential component of most images, there are often times when adding a caption can lift an image.

But there's more to text than mere captions. Think how good it would look if you could engrave an invitation on stone, or carve it into a piece of wood. How good your holiday slideshow could appear if the first frame showed the title written in a sandy beach. Or imagine customizing a photo of a classic car, so that its owner's name was written in gleaming chrome along the side.

We'll look at all these techniques and more in this chapter.

Carving in stone

STONEMASONS TAKE YEARS to learn their craft: after all, the one thing that's certain about carving lettering into stone is that there's no Undo key. Make a mistake and it will cost you dearly.

Fortunately, Elements is rather more forgiving when it comes to carving. All we have to concern ourselves with is arranging the text to its best advantage; we can leave it to Elements to add the bevel effect automatically.

As we'll see here, we don't even need to choose a color for the text. This, too, is added directly by Elements, building on the texture already in the stone for added effect.

We'll demonstrate this technique by adding an inscription to this blank gravestone, in memory of the unfortunate captain of the mutinous ship *Bounty*.

1 Begin by typing your text – centered, for a gravestone. Choose a serif font, such as Caslon Bold, for authenticity. No need to worry about the text color at this stage.

4 Hold **ctrl** and click on the text layer's thumbnail to load up the selection; then hide the text layer, switch to the background layer, and press **ctrl J** to make a new layer from it. Choose Simple Sharp Inner from the Layer Styles palette to make the basic bevel.

2 Now lay out the text for emphasis. Hold `ctrl` `Shift` and press the `>` and `<` keys to make selected text bigger and smaller.

3 In order to distort the text, we first need to make it into a regular layer: choose Layer > Simplify Layer. Now use Free Transform to distort the corner handles in perspective.

5 We now need to modify that bevel, so open Layer > Layer Style > Style Settings. Change the bevel type from Up to Down to make it carved rather than raised. Adding an Inner Glow, using the default settings, brightens the carved lettering as well.

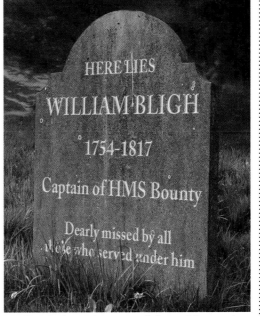

6 To make the carving more realistic, carefully erase the layer with a small Eraser where the grass goes over it. Here, we've also darkened the background layer using the Levels adjustment, and added a new somber sky to complete the spooky graveyard effect.

Neon signs with layer styles

ELEMENTS COMES WITH A BUILT-IN selection of neon styles – called Wow Neon. But they're brash, too bright, and look unconvincing on the screen; they're also set to colors that will look dull and muddy when printed out.

Our approach is rather different. We'll use a Layer Style for the basic neon outline, but will then add our own color glow as a separate layer for a better effect.

As a first step, though, we'll look at how to round off our basic design, above, to give it the sort of smooth corners required for the neon to work properly.

1 After designing your text and any other elements, merge them into a plain white layer. Now apply Gaussian Blur to soften the edges. We've used a 6 pixel radius blur, which applies quite a high degree of smoothing.

4 We need to adjust that glow, so double-click its icon in the Layers palette to open its dialog. Reduce the size of the glow to around 10 pixels, and raise the opacity to 100%; then click the color swatch, and change it to pink.

7 Now for the glow. Make a Magic Wand selection from the original flat layer created in step 2, and feather it by around 12 pixels (*ctrl* *alt* *D*). Make a new layer, and fill the selection with white; then move it behind the neon layer.

8 Press *7* to lock the transparency on this glow layer, then paint each section a darker version of the neon above it. This makes a glow that's more like translucent plastic, making the lettering stronger and more readable.

2 Now for the clever part. Open the Levels adjustment, and drag the white and black sliders together so that they almost touch the gray slider. This tightens up the blur, producing a round-cornered version of the artwork.

3 Select all the elements with the Magic Wand tool and use *ctrl J* to make a new layer from the selection; fill it with black. From the Layer Styles palette, drag a small inner glow onto the new layer.

5 Time for a background. To get rid of the black in the lettering, change the layer's mode from Normal to Screen: the black disappears, leaving just the neon tubing visible; add a drop shadow in Layer Styles for more impact.

6 We want all the elements of our sign to be in different colors. Select each part with the Magic Wand tool, and use *ctrl Shift J* to cut it to a new layer. It will appear with the Layer Styles in place: edit to change the neon color.

9 Need some neon in a hurry? Here's a quicker method. Select all the pieces with the Magic Wand tool after step 2, then use Select>Modify>Contract to make it around 4 pixels smaller. On a new layer, fill the selection with black.

10 Load the Cheat layer styles (see page 245) and apply one of our Neon styles to your outlined text. We've made these in a variety of colors, so you can split the text into different layers and apply a different color to each one.

HOT TIP

The Gaussian Blur/Levels technique used in steps 1 and 2 can be used to smooth out any artwork, adding rounded corners to just about anything. The more you blur, the more rounded the corners will be. Drag the white, gray and black sliders to the left or right to change the thickness of the lettering after blurring it: experiment to see what works best for your design.

Note: you can't change the color of the inner glow in Layer Styles in Elements before version 5.

153

Instant chrome

1 Here's our initial lettering: it's set in the freeware font Deftone Stylus, which is easy to find online. After typing the text, turn it into a regular layer using Layer>Simplify Layer, so we can distort it more easily.

E LEMENTS OFFERS A WIDE VARIETY of ready-made layer styles you can apply to your artwork – among them is a selection of good-looking chrome effects.

As with most layer styles, though, some adjustment is needed before they fit the artwork perfectly. You'll almost always need to adjust the bevel size and the rather over-enthusiastic drop shadow in order to make the style work with your image.

Here, we'll go a step further, and make the chrome reflect its background to match the chrome detail already present on this car.

4 That's far too big a bevel for our purposes. Double-click the Layer Styles icon in the Layers palette, and change the Bevel size to around 8 pixels. Make a note of this number, as we'll need to use it later.

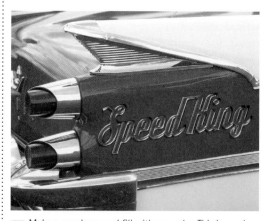

7 Make a new layer, and fill with any color. This is a red sampled from the car body. It looks fairly convincing as it stands, as the inner color matches the car well; but we can make it better still.

2 Use Free Transform to shear the text so that it fits the side of the car. Hold *ctrl* as you drag a corner handle to add a little perspective to it: the lettering gets slightly smaller towards the right-hand side.

3 Now open the Layer Styles palette, and go to the Wow Chrome section. Drag the first style, named Wow Chrome Beveled Edge, onto the layer to apply the effect to the text.

5 We need to reduce the drop shadow amount, too: a far smaller shadow with a smaller offset is needed. By dragging the lighting slider clockwise, we can also get a better chrome effect.

6 Now for the inner part of the lettering. Hold *ctrl* as you click on the layer's thumbnail in the Layers palette to load it up; then choose Select>Modify>Contract, and reduce the size of the selection by 8 pixels.

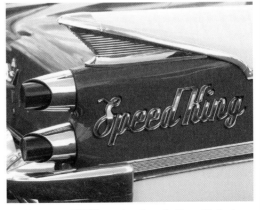

8 Go to the Background layer, and select a portion of the reflection in the fender with the Lasso tool. Make a new layer from the selection, and drag it above the inner color text layer as shown here.

9 Now press *ctrl* *G* to group the reflection with the inner color layer. Use *ctrl* *T* to enter Free Transform, and scale the reflection so that it fills the whole of the lettering. The chrome's now a perfect match to the original car.

HOT TIP

In step 9, you may have some difficulty making the reflection fit the full extent of the inner part of the text. Don't worry if it doesn't quite reach the edges: you can always use the Clone tool to copy any of the texture out to the sides, and any missing portions of the top can easily be painted in by sampling and then painting with a soft edged brush.

No mess pumpkin carving

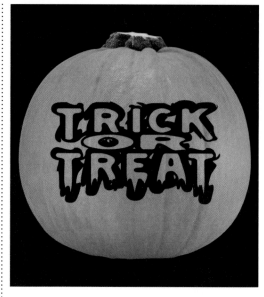

A TRADITIONAL PART OF HALLOWE'EN is the scooping out of pumpkins to make Jack-'o-lanterns. Gone are the days of crudely cut out toothy grins, however, it's now an artform with people spending hours carving intricate images of witches and ghosts in order to out-do their neighbors. This is all very messy and time-consuming, of course.

We can achieve a similar image effect to use in our design, without going near the pumpkin's innards. We'll be using a dingbat style font which, instead of having the standard individual letter characters, has entire words or images. This allows our artwork to be completely re-editable, we can change the motif at any time without having to redo the whole image.

It is an impossible image, of course, there are areas where the text is floating which couldn't really be achieved but we can afford ourselves a little artistic license here as it makes a great party invitation or poster.

1 Here's our pumpkin with the text layer. We've used a dingbat font: the aptly named Trick or Treat which gives us the whole artwork in one go by typing one character, in this case the letter A. At present it's looking somewhat flat and not at all like it's been carved.

4 Create a new layer above the text layer, now load the pumpkin's selection. Contract the selection (under Select > Modify) by around 15 pixels and fill it with 50% Gray. This creates a smaller copy that we can use for the texture inside the pumpkin.

2 Make sure the text layer is active and the Type tool **T** is selected. Go to the Options bar and click the Warped Text button, select Bulge from the menu and choose horizontal as the direction. Now drag the Bend value to the right to try and match the curve of the pumpkin.

3 Choose the Bevels presets from the Layer styles, choose Simple Sharp Outer and apply it to the text layer. The effect needs adjusting so double-click the style indicator to the right of the layer's label. Adjust the bevel size, around 10 pixels for this image, and change the direction to Down.

5 Select the Texturizer filter, set the texture to sandstone and the scaling to 200%. Apply a small amount of Gaussian Blur to soften the effect. Now use Hue/Saturation **ctrl U** set to Colorize and change the color to a warm yellow hue. Press **ctrl D** to deselect.

6 Grab the Dodge tool **O**, set the mode to Highlights and use a large, soft brush to create the impression of a glow radiating from the center. Create a clipping group **ctrl G** with the text layer to hide the excess. Finally we've added a candle and some shading to complete the effect.

Write on the button

BUTTONS, OR BADGES, as they are also known, are often placed on the front of greetings cards bearing a slogan or message for the recipient to wear on their special day (begrudgingly or otherwise). Why not, then, create them virtually to add an extra element of interest to your own designs.

The text on buttons is often written around the edge in a ring. Although there is no built-in function to do this in Elements, it's by no means impossible; as with many things, it's simply a matter of improvisation. The Text Warp function allows us to bend the words to fit. Best of all, being a type layer means it stays editable. You can go back and change the wording at any time whilst still retaining the quality.

1 Begin by creating a new layer. Use the Elliptical Marquee **M** to draw the outline of your button. Remember to hold **Shift** to make it a perfect circle. Fill this with 50% gray for the moment, we can give it a proper color at a later stage. Press **ctrl D** to deselect.

4 The arc doesn't fit because the text is too short. The answer is simply to pad it out using spaces. We can add these before and after the words because we set centred justification. I've hidden the circle and selected the text so the result is visible. The spacing gives us a perfect arc.

2 Select the Type tool **T**, set the alignment to center and click to create a new text layer. We need to split our slogan in two halves as we can only bend the text to a maximum of 180° in one go. Don't worry about the size at this stage, we can adjust that in due course.

3 Select text warp by selecting its icon from the options toolbar. Choose Arc from the style menu, make sure the mode is horizontal and increase the bend to 100%. You can also reposition the text without leaving the dialog. It's looking good but we still need to adjust it slightly.

5 We can now add the second part of our text. This time, we need to bend it in the opposite direction. Open the Warp dialog again, pull the bend slider all the way to the left. Add some extra spacing as we did before. You can also make adjustments with free transform if required.

6 We can add some color to the button itself. This can be done with a Hue/Saturation adjustment or the paint bucket. I've also added some highlights using the dodge tool along with a layer style to round off the edge and add a drop shadow. A thumbs-up in the center completes our effect.

HOT TIP

Not all fonts work well with this technique; because of the effect of the warp tool, wider lettering may become too distorted and give an undesireable result. Try to use a condensed font wherever possible. There are many different styles available from sites on the internet so you will generally be able to find one which fits in with the theme of your design.

Three-dimensional text

WHEN WE WANT TEXT TO STAND OUT we tend to use a bold font, often in a different typeface to the rest of the document. To really draw attention to it we can take it a little further and give it a three-dimensional effect so it jumps off the page at the viewer.

3D text is usually generated by dedicated programs or by using plug-ins; but, as we'll see in the following tutorial, we can create the effect in a few simple steps using the standard Type tool and a crafty trick with selections, layers and the Move tool.

The technique can, of course, be used to add emphasis to your artwork as a heading; you could also use it as part of a montage: creating a sign to place over a store, for example, or as the image above shows: adding some personalised jewelry to a photo.

1 We'll begin by creating a new text layer: grab the Type tool **T**, set the alignment to center and click in the middle of the document to place the cursor. Select a suitable font: larger, rounded styles work especially well. Type out your text, remember to leave some space around it.

4 Turn the original text layer off to avoid confusion. Enter Free Transform **ctrl T**, hold **ctrl alt Shift** and drag the top—left corner handle up a little to add some perpective. Keeping the keys held, drag the top-middle handle to the left to tilt the text back.

7 Make the rear text layer active again. Grab the Burn tool **O**, set a fairly low exposure and choose a large, soft tip. Using a combination of Midtone and Highlight modes, darken the areas that would be in shadow. Hold **alt** to switch to the Dodge tool to add in some extra highlights.

GOLD   GOLD

2 Create a new layer and load up the text's selection. Grab the Gradient tool, choose the copper gradient from the presets palette and set the mode to Reflected. Holding **Shift**, click and drag from the top of the text to the bottom to give a varied range in tones. Press **ctrl D** to deselect.

3 Unsurprisingly, our text does not look very golden at all. We chose the copper gradient because it gives us a good contrast with strong highlights. A Levels adjustment can be used to alter the hues. The technique for this can be found in Chapter 4.

5 Click the original text's thumbnail to make it the active layer then press **ctrl A** to select the canvas. Grab the Move tool **V**, hold down **alt** and, using the cursor keys, nudge once to the right and once upward to copy the pixels. Repeat this several times to create the desired thickness.

6 Press **ctrl J** to create a new layer from the current selection. This will become the face of our text; we can alter this separately from the rest of the effect. This also serves as a mask so we can add shading to the edges of the lettering without affecting the front.

8 Switch back to the top layer and add some additional highlights across the face of the text; being shiny metal, it would pick up random reflections and lighting. We can also add a layer style to add a slight ridge to the front, being a separate layer it doesn't apply to the solid backing.

9 To finish off we've filled the backround with black to set the gold off. A new layer has been created above the text; we've added some small sparkles on the brighter points: these are made with the Crosshatch brush under the Assorted tip presets in the brush palette.

HOT TIP

The addition of shading really helps to bring an image to life. A traditional artist might use different shades of the same color to produce highlight and shadow to their picture; we can brighten or darken the exisiting color using Dodge and Burn – in effect, painting with light. By switching between the midtone and highlight modes, areas can be put into shadow, the color made richer and hotspots added; this is especially good for metal effects. It is, however, worth noting that the results can be fierce if overdone so it's good practise to use a low exposure and build the effect up gradually.

161

Writing in the sand

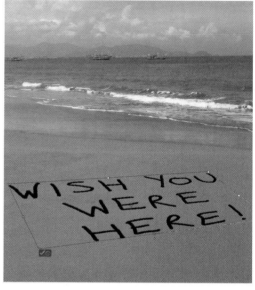

THERE'S SOMETHING ABOUT AN EXPANSE
of smooth, untouched sand that begs
us to carve something into it; this could be a
message of adoration to a loved one or simply a
declaration to prove you were there.

We're going to recreate the effect here using
distortion and layer styles: similar to the stone
carving we made earlier in the chapter, except
we'll create the excess sand around the letters
where it would have been scraped out.

This quick but effective technique lets us
write whatever we want, all without getting a
single grain of sand between our toes; it won't
get washed away, either.

1 Begin by bringing in the text layer. We've hand-written
this to make it more realistic but the effect will work
just as well with a rasterized type layer. Press *ctrl* *T* to
enter Free Transform; hold *ctrl* and drag the corner points to
position the text in perspective on the sand.

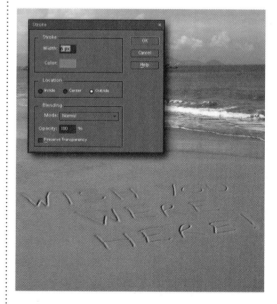

4 Create a new layer and reload the text's selection.
Select Stroke from the Edit menu: set a suitable value
for the width; use the color picker to select a suitable color
from the sand, set the location to outside and apply to create
an outline around the text. Press *ctrl* *D* to deselect.

2 Load the layer's selection then hide it by clicking its eyeball icon. Make the background layer active again and press *ctrl J* to copy the selection to a new layer. Change the layer's blend mode to Multiply to make it darker against the background whilst still retaining its texture.

3 Apply the Simple Sharp Inner bevel preset from the Effects palette. Double-click the layer's style icon in the layers palette to open the control dialog. Lower the bevel value and adjust the lighting angle and set the direction to Down to create a carved appearance.

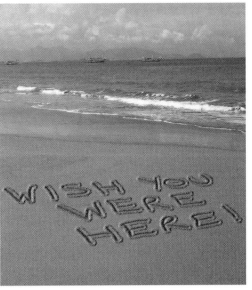

5 Apply a small amount of Noise to add some texture, we used the uniform, monochromatic setting with an amount of around 12% here. Add a Simple Inner bevel and decrease its width a little, this time keep the direction set to Up to give it a raised appearance.

6 Set the blend mode to Dissolve and lower the opacity to give the outline a broken up grainy effect. We've also lowered the base text's opacity and darkened the two layers a little using Levels giving the impression of the wet underlying sand showing through.

HOT TIP

The Dissolve blend mode is great for creating grainy effects or for eroding parts of the image. Unfortunately, because it uses the opacity of the layer to determine the intensity you cannot soften the pixels by applying a blur. To get around the problem first create a new layer beneath the target layer then merge them together. The resulting layer preserves the effect which will no longer be affected by blurring or further changes to the opacity.

Chop and change

1 We'll start by creating the cut—away effect to show the background beneath the fabric. Grab the Type tool **T** and place the text; the color is not important as we'll only be using it as a template. We've used a heavy font here for clarity but most weights will work just as well.

IT'S FAIRLY SAFE TO ASSUME that you wouldn't consider mercilessly plunging a scalpel into a priceless painting solely to advertise your upcoming art exhibition; unless, of course, it was one of those avant-garde affairs, in which case it would be positively frowned upon if you didn't. That aside, it's surprising how often we start hacking into our images without a moment's thought and, whilst we do have the safety of the undo command, there are far better ways to take chunks out of our artwork.

By using a combination of text layers, clipping masks and layer styles we can create the effect of words being cut out of a piece of material (or almost any other substance) to reveal a surface beneath. What's more, this technique is completely editable as we never actually cut into the image; we simply create the illusion of doing so.

4 That's looking a lot better. Before we add the cut-out text itself we'll make some space for it on the artwork. Grab the Move tool **V** and drag the text down towards the bottom. Because the style is applied to the text layer the effect also moves; so we can position it wherever we want.

7 We need to reposition the new text but this time we want the pattern to move with it. Click the text layer's label (not the thumbnail), now hold **ctrl** and click the texture layer's label to form a group. We can also make this more permanent by clicking the chain icon to link them together.

2 We can bring in the image layer to use as our revealed background now: this is placed above our text layer with which we've created a clipping group by pressing *ctrl* *G*. In doing this we've hidden all but the area where our text is visible.

3 It's not looking too convincing at the moment; there's no sense of depth. Make the text layer active and go to the Effects palette: select Layer Styles and from there choose the Inner Shadows from the menu. Finally, select the Low preset by pressing Apply or by double-clicking its icon.

At the time of writing, the current version of Elements does not have the option to adjust the inner shadow layer style. Although the default settings work well in our example, they may not look as good on different image sizes. To compensate for this we've included a collection of presets on the accompanying CD. Information on how to install them can be found in the CD content section at the back of the book.

5 Holding *alt*, click and drag the text layer's thumbnail to the top of the layer stack. This creates a copy without having to relink the original's clipping mask. Now duplicate the background layer and drag it above the new text. Finally, create a clipping group with the two new layers.

6 We still have the previous style set from the copy. Right-click the style indicator icon and select Clear Layer Style. Now go back to the Effects palette and select Drop Shadows from the drop-down list. The Low preset works well here.

8 Press *ctrl* *T* to enter Free Transform, we can now move and rotate the text and its overlay into position in unison. The bounding box seems far too large compared to the text but remember, we are transforming the entire clipped texture layer. Press *Enter* to apply the changes.

9 With everything in place we can change the text without having to reapply the effects and textures. Double-click the type layer to change edit it. This works both ways, of course: you could just as easily change the styles or replace the backgrounds leaving the text intact.

165

Image size

UNDERSTANDING IMAGE SIZE is a conundrum that puzzles many Elements users. Just what is 'dots per inch', and how do they relate to the megapixel sizes quoted by the manufacturers of digital cameras? What resolution is required for printing, or saving files for the web?

Image size is traditionally measured in dots per inch (dpi), even if you're accustomed to working in centimeters. You can, of course, work in centimeters per inch, but we'll stick to dpi here to be in tune with the convention.

Computer monitors typically display images at 72 dpi. This means 72 pixels across and 72 down, which amounts to 5,184 physical pixels in each square inch of screen space. This is the resolution you should work at when designing for the web. In Elements, when you view an image at '100%', you're seeing it at 72 dpi: in other words, each pixel in the image precisely matches one pixel on the screen. Viewing images at a smaller size - say, 50% - means that each pixel on the screen displays an average of the colour of four pixels in the original document. If you zoom in further, to say 800%, you can see each pixel with much greater clarity; they'll clearly appear as squares.

Commercial printing uses only four basic colors: cyan, magenta, yellow and black. All other colours are simulated by overprinting these four. The bigger the printed dot, the more of that colour is seen; so if in one region there are equal sized cyan and yellow dots, you'll see green. If the cyan dots are twice the size as the yellow, the result will be turquoise. Clearly, these dots need to be tiny if we're not going to notice them; and the smoother the paper, the smaller the dots can be. Newspapers print at around 100 dpi; glossy magazines at around 250 dpi, occasionally more.

When printing on an inkjet printer, however, the color is made up from arrays of tiny dots of equal size. The more dots that are clustered together, the stronger the density of that color. Inkjet printers typically print at 1200 dpi, which produces a smooth tonal range with a dot that's barely perceptible. That doesn't mean you need to work at 1200 dpi in Elements: a size of 150 dpi is more than adequate for getting excellent color prints from most inkjet printers.

Digital cameras capture pixels on a CCD chip: the better the camera, the more pixels on the chip, and so the higher the resolution at which the image can be

| Original image, composed of smooth colors | Image converted to square pixels on computer monitor | Image printed using dot clusters on inkjet printer | Image printed using different sized dots in magazine |

recorded. If a camera is quoted as having an image size of 3.2 megapixels, it will produce images that measure 2048 pixels wide by 1536 pixels high. Multiplying these values together – the total number of pixels in the image – produces 3,145,728 pixels overall, or rather over three million pixels: and that's what the 3.2 megapixel name refers to.

If printed in a newspaper, a 3.2 megapixel camera could produce a high quality image at up to about 10 x 8 inches. The same image in a glossy magazine could be used at up to around half an A4 page; if printed any larger than this, the pixels in the image would be larger than the printed dot size, and we'd start to see ungainly pixellation in the finished result. When shown on a web page, however, the same image would easily fill the entire area of a huge 30 inch monitor.

The software that comes with most flatbed scanners tends, confusingly, to offer the ability to adjust both the size and the resolution of scans. In fact, these both amount to the same thing; it's the number of pixels captured in total that counts, not the relative dimensions. The easy solution is to scan an image at the size you're going to want to use it, at a resolution appropriate for the medium on which it's going to end up - printed out, or on the screen. Err on the high side: you can always reduce an image's size in Elements, but you can't easily increase it without loss of quality. Bear in mind, though, that the larger the file, the slower it will be to work on in Elements.

The Image Size dialog in Elements has the ability to resample images to any size and resolution you choose. But if you uncheck the 'Resample Image' button, it will adjust the size and resolution together. This is a useful method for turning, say, digital camera captures – which typically have a resolution of 180 dpi – into screen-ready files with a resolution of 72 dpi.

The camera never lies, we're told. But sometimes we wish it would be less scrupulously honest. The photo above is a charming shot of two people who love each other; but how much nicer it would be for them if some of the ravages of time were washed away. And perhaps they could be in a better location, as well.

9

People and animals

THE LATE, GREAT W. C. FIELDS told us never to work with children or animals. Sound advice, for sure. But we photograph people and pets more than just about any other subject, so we need to know how to work with them in Elements.

In this chapter we'll look at how to fix blemishes, how to reverse the ageing process, and how to make people look slimmer. We'll also explore several other everyday tasks to enhance our images – as well as some tasks, such as swapping heads, that are far from commonplace. Whether you're making a birthday card for a friend, or simply enhancing a family photo, we've got the solutions to make the job easier.

Heads on bodies

ONE OF THE MOST IMPRESSIVE tricks we can play in Elements is to place a celebrity's head on the body of a family member. It's easy enough to come across suitable celebrities on the internet: one of the best places is Wikipedia, which includes thousands of celebrities that are free to use, in its Wikimedia Commons department.

The trick to making this technique work lies in choosing a head shot at the right angle to work with your image. Don't worry about the size and the color, as we can easily fix that later; all that matters for now is that the orientation is as close as you can find to the head in the original photograph.

1 We found this picture of Arnold Schwarzenegger on the Wikipedia website. It's just the right angle to fit on the body of the dad in our family shot. The first step is to cut it out from its background, using any of the techniques described in Chapter 1.

4 Although we got the size and angle right in the previous step, Arnie's coloring didn't match the rest of the photograph. The best way to adjust the color of the new head is to use the Levels adjustment, which also allows us to correct the contrast.

2 Drag the cutout head into the image where you want it to appear. To make it roughly the right size, it helps if you position it next to the target head, rather than on top: by being able to see both at the same time, we can be sure to get the size right.

3 Rotate and further scale the head as necessary using Free Transform, and place it on top of the original head. Take your time with this step, as it's the key to making the montage work. Here, we've rotated the head anticlockwise slightly for a more appealing look.

5 There's a hard line under Arnie's chin that needs to be dealt with. The simplest way of removing this is to use a small, soft-edged eraser to smooth out the join; for more control, use an adjustment layer mask, as described in Chapter 3.

6 Finally, we need to remove the pieces of the original head that are still visible behind Arnie. On the background layer, use the Clone tool to sample pieces of the background and paint them in to cover up the original ear and other features that stuck out.

HOT TIP

When you cut out a head to use in a montage, don't cut it directly beneath the chin: take as much neck as you can as well. This will help you to blend the head into the new body, as it's easier to fade one neck smoothly into another than it is to blur the line beneath a hard chin.

171

Photomerge: faces

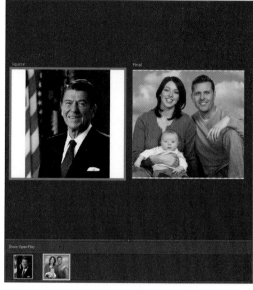

O N THE PREVIOUS PAGES we looked at how to place a head on a different body. Elements 6 brings us a new technology, Photomerge, which automates the process.

Unlike the previous method, Photomerge doesn't require us to cut out the original head first: it can recognize a head shape within an image, even against a background as complicated as the one behind Ronald Reagan in this example.

The technology isn't perfect, and it can be a little tricky to control: but it's a quick way of moving heads between images, and can be a lot of fun to play around with.

1 To begin, make sure the head you want to copy into the mix is on the left in the palette bin – drag it there if it isn't in place already. Now choose New > Photomerge Faces. You'll be prompted to drag the final image into the space on the right.

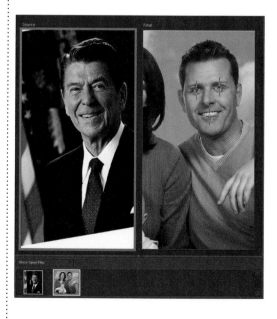

4 Move the markers on either image and press Align Photos again to correct the distortion. It can take a few tries to get it right: you need to move the markers in the opposite direction than what you'd expect in order to undistort the face.

2 Now click on the Alignment tool within the Photomerge dialog, and three numbered crosshairs will appear. Drag these onto the first image – one for each of the eyes, and one for the mouth. Accurate placement of these markers is essential to making this technique work, so zoom in first.

3 Now place the markers on the second face in corresponding positions, and click the Align Photos button. As we can see, this has produced a rather distorted shot of Reagan in the first frame; we need to adjust the positions of the markers to correct this.

5 Now for the fun part. Grab the Pencil tool, and draw over Reagan's face. In a couple of seconds, the face will appear superimposed over the family photograph. As we can see, though, it's also darkened up the sky behind the figure, and Reagan's ear overlaps the original ear.

6 We can't do much more editing here: but pressing Done will produce a new document with two layers – the original family shot, and the family with Reagen placed over the top. Eraser parts of this layer, or use an adjustment layer mask (see Chapter 3) to make a better fit.

Cosmetic surgery: healing

HERE'S A GRUMPY TEENAGER. So what else is new? Well, this teenager has a reason to be grumpy: she's about to go on a hot date and her face is covered in acne spots. (To be fair to the original model, we should point out that we added these blemishes ourselves.)

A two week course of antibiotics could clear this up – but we have a quicker method. Using the Healing Brush and the Spot Healing Brush – how appropriate – we can lose those ugly spots with just a few clicks.

Using this innovative tool isn't always plain sailing, however, as we'll see here: when the blemishes are close to an edge, unwanted effects can occur. This is the best way to prevent those errors.

1 Choose the Spot Healing Brush (shortcut: **J**) and make sure it's set to use a hard-edged brush. This seems contradictory: you'd expect a soft brush to blend in better. But that's not how this one works. Paint roughly over the spot on the forehead, and you'll see where you've painted.

4 When we paint over the spot on her left cheek, however, something goes wrong. The tool has inadvertently sampled the edge of her face, producing what looks like an ugly scar. There are occasions when the Spot Healing Brush doesn't have a clear enough region from which to sample.

2 As soon as you release the mouse button, the Spot Healing Brush does something extraordinary: it samples the texture around the place you painted, and blends that texture in perfectly with the surroundings. Our first spot disappears instantly.

3 We can carry on in the same manner, painting over each spot in turn on the girl's right cheek. Paint just enough area to cover the spot, and no more, for the tool to perform at its best.

5 Undo that last step and, instead, switch to the regular Healing Brush. This works in a slightly different way: first, we hold **alt** and click a point from which to sample the texture – the forehead works well – and then paint over the spot. Now, it disappears as we wish it to.

6 The spot above the lip presents a different problem. The spot is just too close to the mouth. Before healing, make a selection that includes the spot, but which stops at the top of the mouth. Now, when we use the tool, it won't act outside that area – and so the mouth is left intact.

HOT TIP

The Healing Brush is a hugely powerful tool. Use it to remove birds from the sky, beetles from a rock, or even commonly unwanted picture elements such as telegraph wires and signposts. The really clever thing about it is that you don't need to match the lighting, or even the color: only the texture is sampled, and is blended in perfectly with the background.

Cosmetic surgery: weight loss

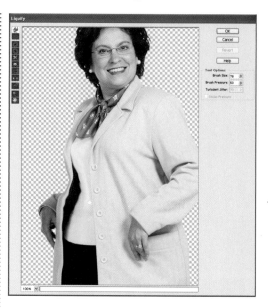

1 Use Filter > Distort > Liquify to enter the Liquify dialog. The default tool is Warp: use this to push the waist in, as we start to slim our model. Use a large brush size: small brushes will simply create additional wrinkles, and that's the very thing we want to get rid of.

THIS IS THE WEIGHT LOSS PROGRAM the world's been waiting for: no diets, no exercise, just a ten-minute workout with the Liquify filter.

In order to make this procedure work properly, you'll need to cut out your image from its background. Otherwise, the existing background will be too distorted to look realistic.

We'll use this image of a woman who, while not being obese, would perhaps value the opportunity to shed a few pounds.

4 Don't forget such details as slimming the ankles – again, by pushing in from either side. It's details like this that make all the difference between a convincing montage and one that looks fake. But be careful not to get carried away, if you want a realistic result.

2 It's easy to distort the hands by accident when smearing them with Liquify. The solution is to stick with a large brush size, and click and drag directly on the hand. With luck, the entire hand should move as one; switch to a smaller brush to clean up if necessary.

3 Push the bottom and the tops of the legs into the center to make them appear slimmer. Again, be careful not to distort the hands.

5 The face is trickier. With a smaller brush size, push the chin and neck inwards. Switch to the Bloat tool and press on the eyes to make them slightly larger: this accentuates the features, and makes the whole face look less chubby.

HOT TIP

Use the square bracket keys and **[** to **]** make the brush size smaller and larger. The size changes very slowly when you do this; to speed it up, hold the *Shift* key as you press the bracket keys.

Although we've looked at making realistic changes here, there's no limit to what you can do with the Liquify filter. Try changing expressions, or growing devil's horns out of someone's head.

Age and youth

H OW OFTEN HAVE YOU TAKEN a
photograph of an elderly relative, only
for them to complain that they look much older
than they expected? We all have an idea of
how we appear to others, and the image in our
minds is often several years younger than we
really are.

If only there were a way to take the years
off without resorting to expensive and painful
surgery. Well, there is: we can harness the
power of Elements to darken hair, remove
wrinkles, tighten that sagging chin and present
an altogether more youthful appearance.

We've taken the approach to extremes in this
tutorial; generally, you'd only want to remove a
few lines and creases. And perhaps fix that chin.
Oh, and you may as well darken the hair a little
while you're at it...

1 The first thing to do is to tighten that sagging chin. Go
to Filter > Distort > Liquify, and use the default tool to
push the chin up and in. Start with a large brush: you can
use the **[** and **]** keys to make the brush size smaller and
larger.

4 The Spot Healing Brush would have trouble with
wrinkles close to facial features. Instead, switch to the
regular Healing Brush, and **alt** click on the center of the
forehead to set the source point. Now when you paint over
the wrinkles they'll heal perfectly. Remember the bags under
the eyes, and the wrinkles beneath the chin.

2 Select the hair with the Lasso tool, and apply a 5 pixel feather to it (*ctrl* *alt* *D*) to soften the edge. Make this into a new layer with *ctrl* *J*, and open the Levels dialog. Drag the middle gray triangle to the right to darken the hair.

3 Use the Spot Healing Brush (*J*) to paint out the lines on the forehead. It will sample texture from around the area you paint, patching the lines perfectly. Because there's so much clear forehead texture around the wrinkles, the tool works well here.

5 Let's address the hair loss that our unfortunate senior citizen has suffered. Rebuilding hair is tricky, but here's a simple solution. Select the top half of the hair, and use *ctrl* *J* to make a new layer from it. Drag it down so it covers more of the forehead.

6 Switch to the Smudge tool, and choose a soft-edged brush – or one of the star-shaped custom brushes. With a pressure of around 70%, smudge the new hair both up into the original, and down onto the forehead. This tool makes it easy to blend the new hair in with the old. Our rejuvenated favorite uncle is now complete.

179

Adding people to the scene

THE SCENE IS AN ENGAGEMENT PARTY: the blushing bride-to-be shares a glass of champagne with her future husband. Such a shame her father couldn't be there to enjoy the occasion... but, thanks to Elements, he can be. Adding people to a scene is just one of the techniques every Elements montage artist should be familiar with.

2 After a lot of painting in and out, pressing **X** to swap between foreground and background colors, we're able to tuck Dad firmly behind the couple. Since they're both holding glasses, though, we need to make them slightly transparent: and this is how it's done. Still on the

Adjustment layer mask, set the foreground color to white (to paint the figure back in), and set the opacity to just 20%. Now, when we paint over the glasses area with a hard-edged brush, we reveal a hint of his shirt pattern as seen through the champagne glasses.

1 We'll start by cutting the bride's father out from his original background (we've already done this for you in the version included on the CD). Once he's been moved into the engagement photo, the first step is to use Free Transform to make him the right size. Again, we've done this for you. Next, we need to place him behind the happy couple. Although we could do this with the Eraser tool, it's far easier using a custom layer mask – see page 40 for how this is done. Once he's grouped with his Adjustment layer, we can paint on that layer to hide him behind the couple.

see page 40

3 The final problem is one of coloring. The photo of Dad was too blue in comparison with the bride and groom photo. So switch to Dad's layer, and open the Levels adjustment dialog. Begin with the Blue channel (*ctrl* **3**), dragging the middle gray slider to the right to reduce the amount of blue in the image. Then switch to the composite RGB channel, and drag the same slider to the right to reduce the brightness overall. Finally, switch to the Red channel (*ctrl* **1**) and this time drag the slider slightly to the left, to increase the amount of red a little.

HOT TIP

Using the layer mask technique makes it far easier to slot a figure into a scene. But be sure to pay attention to the colors: it's rare that the skin-tones from two different photographs will match, and it's here that most montage artists fall down badly. It can help to think backwards: if an image is too green, try adding blue and red rather than simply taking out the green.

Eyes wide shut

W E MAY HAVE the ability to take as many pictures as we want with our digital cameras, but unfortunately we still can't guarantee they'll be great shots every time, as is the case with our example. While the kids obliged us with a lovely pose for the portrait, one of them blinked at precisely the wrong moment.

All is not lost, however: using another picture (shown in the inset) of the girl in which her eyes are open, we can copy them from one image to the other and blend them in seamlessly, rescuing our photo from the delete pile.

1 The second image has been brought into the document as a new layer, and we've lowered the opacity to enable us to see the original image below. The girl is facing slightly to the right in the first photo but to the left in the second, so we need to flip the layer horizontally. We can now use Free Transform to scale and position and rotate the layer, matching it as closely as possible. Don't spend too much time trying to get it perfect first time; we can make finer adjustments later.

3 With just the eyes overlaid on our original photo we can see that, whilst it's a very close match, we still need to do a little fine-tuning. Enter Free Transform mode again; because we're now working on a smaller area, we can make more accurate adjustments. In this case all that's needed is a very slight rotation and a nudge upward. These changes can make all the difference. Our brains are trained to read faces, and any anomolies can be glaringly obvious.

2 Now we have the layer in place we can bring its opacity back up to 100%. At this point we could use the eraser to remove the excess from the image; there is a far better way, however. Grab the Selection Brush **A** and choose a large,

soft tip. Paint in a loose mask-like selection over and around the eyes, now press *ctrl* *J* to create a copy of the eyes on a new layer. We can hide or discard the previous image as it's no longer needed.

In this example it was fortunate that the two faces were shot at very similar angles, enabling us to copy and position them as a single layer. You won't always have this luxury but the chances are good that one of the eyes will fit with very little adjustment. This can be duplicated and flipped to create the pair.

It's also worth noting that in some instances you may need to copy more of the face, particularly if the subject's expression is dramatically different in each image; the shape of the features will change slightly and could affect the realism of the result.

4 We're almost done – there's just a bit of tidying up to be carried out. Because the second image has slightly different lighting, some areas are too bright for the original photo. Select a medium size, soft eraser **E**, lower its opacity

and use its edge to feather out the area around the periphery of the eyes to bring back some of the original shadowing. As she has such a nice smile in the other photo, we've added that in the same way to finish the image off.

183

Warhol style pop art

THE ICONIC IMAGE OF MARILYN MONROE is one of Andy Warhol's most famous works. He used the screen printing process to transfer photographs to canvas which were then overlaid with blocks of heavy, garish color giving them the now familiar impressionistic style. The aim was to streamline the process to enable the images to be mass-produced whilst each would be slightly different to the last.

We can recreate the effect surprisingly easily: by simplifying the photo to purely black and white we can then build up the image using individual layers of color – a digital version of screen-printing, as it were. Because we're using adjustment layers we can, of course, edit the image time after time, changing its colors or altering the level of detail.

1 Start by isolating the woman from the background; the best choice for this image is the Magic Wand **W**. Disable the contiguous option to select all the black areas at once; tidy any stray areas on the face with the Selection Brush **A**. Inverse the selection and copy to a new layer.

4 Add another color layer the same as before but select a yellow for the hair. Again, paint over the mask to reveal the color. Now add a white layer for the eyes and teeth: this time set the mode to Overlay. The order of the layers can be important as the blend modes affect surrounding layers too.

2 Add a Threshold adjustment layer above the new layer. The initial result is too strong and we've lost a lot of the detail. Slowly drag the slider to the left until all but the main features are visible — make sure the eyes are fairly well defined. Press *ctrl* *G* to create a clipping group.

3 Create a Solid Color adjustment layer above the Threshold layer. Select a suitable color for the skin-tone and set the blend mode to Darken. Now click the layer's mask thumbnail and fill it with black to hide the effect. Using a hard brush, paint in white to reveal the areas of color.

5 Create a red layer for the lips, this will need to be set to Lighten. Paint in the eye-shadow and the necklace. If you're finding it tricky to see which parts should be a certain color, hold *alt* and click the original photo's visibility icon; this toggles the effect on and off by hiding the layers.

6 Duplicate the head layer and place it at the top of the stack. Set its blend mode to Color Burn and lower the opacity to 50%. Create a new Threshold adjustment, and this time drag the slider to the right to increase the black detail. Add a plain colored background to complete the effect.

HOT TIP

Holding *alt* whilst selecting an adjustment layer from the menu in the Layers palette forces its option dialog to appear. From here you can rename it, choose to create it as a clipping mask and set the blend mode during the creation process.

185

Public enemy No. 1

WILD WEST STYLE WANTED POSTERS have always made great novelty gifts – unless you're really an outlaw being chased across Dodge City, that is. There's a never ending amount of reasons that can be put on the poster as to why that person is being sought: for being the best Dad, for being a perfect student or on a landmark birthday, to name but a few.

Today's posters generally use a photo for the subject's picture, often sepia toned to give the aged appearance; however, photography was still in its infancy back then, which meant they would have been really expensive to produce in this form, so most would have been made using a sketch of the person instead. That's just what we're going to do here, except we'll start with a photo, of course.

1 Here's our blank poster. The technique for creating this can be found in Chapter 5. First we need to add our rascal into the image. We've used the Place command to open and automatically fit the image into our document. We can use the handles to scale him down further.

4 Merge the two layers using **ctrl E**, and set the blend mode to Linear Burn. This hides the white allowing the paper to show through and also gives a slightly warmer tone to the effect. It's still a little too sharp so we'll soften it a little: the Blur More command is perfect for this.

5 Create a new layer. Select the Rectangular Marquee **M** and draw a narrow horizontal box around 3/4 of the poster's width, just beneath the man. Fill with a dark brown. Hold **alt ctrl Shift**, and click and drag to create a copy above his head and lower the opacity a little.

2 Desaturate the image with *ctrl* *Shift* *U* and press *ctrl* *J* to duplicate the layer. Invert the copy by pressing *ctrl* *I* and set its blend mode to Color Dodge. The cowboy image will now have turned completely white; this is what we want.

3 Open the Gaussian Blur filter, make sure the preview is enabled and begin to adjust the value up or down. As you do so you will see the image become more defined. We found a value of 5 pixels worked well with this image. Create a clipping group *ctrl* *G* to tighten up the edges.

6 Select the Type tool *T*, choose a suitable font – we've used one from dafont.com named Post Office. Click above the top line you created to create a new text layer. Type the WANTED! headline; now hold *ctrl* to access the transform controls and scale the text to fit.

7 Add the rest of the text in the same way as before. Lower the opacity of the text to match the frame borders. As a final touch we've drawn a couple of nails to hold it up and added a shadow to make it a little more three-dimensional.

HOT TIP

When you choose a color via the color picker, you can select it from any part of an open image within Elements. Move the cursor outside of the dialog and it will change to the eye-dropper cursor. Click to select the color from the point beneath it.

187

Bobblehead caricature

TYPICALLY, CARICATURES FOCUS on one or more of the subject's features which are then drawn greatly exaggerated. Bobbleheads, on the other hand, have huge versions of the person's head atop a ludicrously small body. The head and body are usually connected by a spring, which, when tapped causes the head to bob about – hence the name. These collectable models generally depict sporting personalities but some movie stars also have their own jittering counterparts.

As we'll see in the following example we can, of course, create our own digital versions. This simple yet effective technique can be used to make great humorous greetings cards or gifts for friends and relatives.

1 Our singer is already on a separate layer so begin by loading up his selection. Select the Freehand Lasso tool, holding **alt** **Shift**, carefully draw a line starting from his ear and down around his jawline. Close this off with a loosely drawn area around the rest of his head.

4 Now we've toned down his features we can give him a real plastic appearance with the Plastic Wrap filter. Experiment with the slider adjustments until you have the desired effect; we want to keep it fairly subtle. As before, apply this to the body layer as well.

Smart Blur

OK

Cancel

100%

Radius 9.0

Threshold 30.0

Quality: Low

Mode: Normal

2 Copy the head to a new layer with **ctrl J**. Click the original body layer's thumbnail and use free transform to scale it down to a suitably comical size; we want to emphasise the face whilst retaining the body detail. You may also want to tilt the head slightly to the left.

3 We need to make him look more like a a model: open the Smart Blur filter, and leave the quality set to low. Adjust the Radius and Threshold to smooth out the detail but retain a suitable amount of clarity to the features. Switch to the body and reapply the effect by pressing **ctrl F**.

5 We need to have the hand with the microphone in front of his head. Hide the head layer for now and make sure the body layer is active. Draw a selection around the hand using the Lasso, copy it to a new layer and move it above the head in the Layers palette by dragging its thumbnail.

6 Here's our finished image. We've increased the saturation a little and added some shading under his head with the Burn tool; this helps to bond the image together. We've also given him a shadow to place him properly – see Chapter 5 for more on how to do this.

HOT TIP

The results from the Plastic Wrap filter can vary immensely depending on the lighting and quality of the source image. If you are having difficulty producing a balanced effect, try duplicating the layer(s) before applying the filter. Doing this enables you to fine tune the result by altering the opacity and blend mode to produce a more subtle effect.

189

All in the mind

WHAT'S ON A YOUNG GIRL'S MIND? Hard to say with any certainty – but we can make a safe bet that it would include teddy bears, ponies and candy. We're going to show these interests graphically, by lifting the top of her head and placing all these items inside.

The only thing we have to concern ourselves with here is the correct order of the layers in the stack. In order to place everything inside the head, we need to position the objects between the face and the interior – which means splitting that rim into two, so the front half will remain in front.

1 The first step is to draw the inside of the head, as an ellipse. But Elements has no tools for drawing an ellipse at an angle; we'll make it easy for ourselves by first drawing a circle, on a new layer. Here, we've filled it with blue and set it to Multiply so we can see through it.

4 Load up the ellipse selection by holding **ctrl** and clicking on its thumbnail in the Layers palette. Use Select > Modify > Contract to make the selection around 8 pixels smaller; then, using the Burn tool, darken the interior so that it looks hollow.

2 Use *ctrl* **T** to enter Free Transform, and rotate and squeeze the circle so it becomes an ellipse at the right angle. Don't stretch it all the way out to the right: remember, her head is actually some distance inside all that hair.

3 Fill the ellipse with a flesh color sampled from her skin, and change its mode back to Normal. With the ellipse selected, move to the girl's layer and press *Backspace* to delete her head from this area; then deselect, and erase any hair still visible above the ellipse.

HOT TIP

All the elements inside this head are behind the head layer. If we wanted the horse's nose, for instance, to poke in front of the head, then we'd need to select the nose and use *ctrl* **J to make a new layer from it. When we bring this to the top of the layer stack, we can move the horse and its nose together, and position them as we wish.**

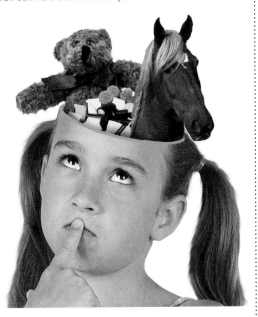

5 Don't deselect. Instead, inverse the selection using *ctrl* *Shift* **I**, so that just the pink rim is selected. Hold *alt* *Shift* as you trace a loop around the front half of the rim; press *ctrl* **J** to make a new layer from this section, and bring it to the front.

6 Send the head interior to the bottom of the layer stack, so that it's placed behind the head. We can now add all our objects as we like, behind the head layer, and they'll appear to be inside it. Add a little shading, on a new layer, to complete the effect.

191

Dog in a basket

H AIR AND FUR are among the trickiest
materials to cut out in Elements. Take
this photograph of a dog, for instance: we can
see its wispy, shaggy fur well enough, but how
on earth are we supposed to cut it away from
all that grass?

The solution, as ever, is to cheat. Rather
than even attempting to use one of the many
selection methods to trace around the fur, we'll
do a smooth cutout and then redraw the fur
using the Smudge tool.

We're going to practice our technique with a
dog's fur here, but we can use the same method
on people: it's far easier to recreate the effect
of flyaway hair using the Smudge tool than it is
to try to cut it from a complex background.

1 Begin by cutting out the dog from the background, using
the Lasso or Selection Brush, or any of the selection
tools described in Chapter 1. No need to be too accurate
here - you don't need to trace over every strand of hair; but
cut inside the hair rather than outside it, so that no grass is
included in the selection.

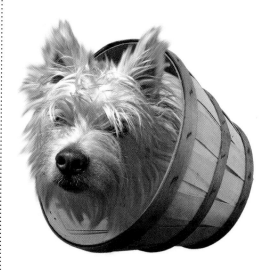

4 Continue all the way around the dog, pulling out clumps
of fur with the Smudge tool. Refer to the original photo,
if you like – but it's just as easy (and just as convincing) to
guess at what the fur will look like. If you find 80% pressure
is too great, reduce it for a smaller effect.

2 We've decided to place our dog in this basket, for no reason other than it looks cute there. To make this work, we've first copied the front half of the basket to a new layer: with this section in front of the dog, and the original behind, it's easy to manipulate the two so that it looks as if the dog's sitting inside.

3 Switch to the Smudge tool, set to a pressure of around 80%. The key to making this easier lies in choosing the correct brush for this tool: a Spatter brush, which is one of the default Elements brushes, is perfect. Drag out clumps of fur around the edge of the dog, following the direction in which it would naturally grow.

HOT TIP

This technique works best if you have a pressure sensitive graphics tablet: it's far easier to tweak out the fur if you can vary the pressure, rather than relying on the uniform pressure provided by a mouse alone.

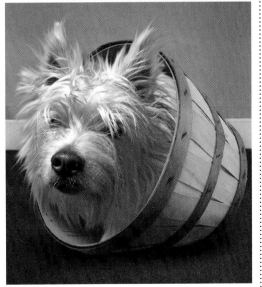

5 We now need to tweak out a few individual strands of fur for added realism. Still using the Smudge tool, choose a small, soft brush – around 3 pixels in diameter – and pull out the strands one at a time. This greatly increases the realism of the fur.

6 The technique works well enough against a white background, but it really comes into its own when we place the entire assembly into a real room. Paint in shadows beneath the basket and inside it, under the dog, for a more realistic appearance.

Tiffs, JPEGs and the rest

ONE OF THE MOST BAFFLING issues facing the Elements user is the Save As dialog. It should be straightforward: after all, all you want to do is save your file. So why are there so many options? Here are all the main file types you'll see listed, with an explanation of what they're used for.

The formats you'll need

Photoshop (.psd) is the full file you're working on, containing all the layers, styles, effects, adjustment layers and so on. Save in this format when you want to carry on working on your image.

JPEG (.jpg) stands for Joint Photography Experts' Group, and is a highly compressed format that's good for delivering images over the internet. There's a trade-off between high quality and small file sizes: the higher the JPEG value, the more faithful the image will be to the original, but the bigger the file.

TIFF (.tif) stands for Tagged Image File Format, and this was the file format of choice before JPEGs came along. It's not lossy, as JPEGs are, and the resulting files are much bigger; unlike JPEGs, it can contain both layers and selection channels, so is good for exporting images for use in other applications.

JPEG 2000 (.jpf, .jp2) is a newer version of JPEGs that offers better quality, and also supports selection channels. Most web browsers can't read this format, though, so it's no good for internet delivery.

Compuserve GIF (.gif) stands for Graphics Interchange Format, and is a format introduced in 1987 and used primarily for web delivery. It includes only a very limited range of colors, so images will look very rough; on the plus side, it can contain multiple frames of an animation.

PNG (.png) stands for Portable Network Graphics, and is a more recent format intended for internet delivery. It's not that commonly used, although it does support transparency, and so is useful for web designers.

Photoshop Raw (.raw) is the high-end, high bandwidth version of images captured by professional quality digital cameras. Many professional photographers prefer this format for its extended tonal range.

Photoshop PDF (.pdf) stands for Portable Document Format, which was developed so that one complex file including text and graphics could be viewed identically on multiple computer platforms. The Photoshop Elements version is there to provide compatability.

The formats you won't need, but may as well know about

BMP, or 'Bitmap' (.bmp) is a format designed for use internally by MS-DOS and, later, Windows. It's hugely wasteful, resulting in enormous file sizes.

Photoshop EPS (.eps) stands for Encapsulated PostScript, and is the format images used to be converted into for color printing. It's now rarely used, except for jobs in unusual color spaces – such as those to be printed in CMYK plus a special Pantone color.

Scitex CT (.sct) was a high-end reprographic format in the early days of desktop publishing. CT stands for 'continuous tone'.

Targa (.tga) was a graphics format used on graphics cards for IBM compatible PCS. Many games still create screenshots in Targa format; the online game Second Life accepts textures in this format, which supports transparency.

The formats you don't even need to know about

PICT (.pct) and **PCX (.pcx)** were internal formats used by early Mac and DOS computers respectively. Along with Photo Creation Format and Pixar, they're only provided as options in case you want to open graphics files created many years ago on ancient computer systems.

A simple still life, above: the fruit bowl, candlestick and bottle are all on separate layers, as are the table and the curtain behind. Adding the shadows was straightforward enough: but the scene is dull and looks unrealistic. Adding reflections to that wood surface really bring this picture to life, giving it an extra dimension.

10

Shiny surfaces

GLASS, METAL AND WATER all have one thing in common: they're shiny. Which means that any objects placed on these surfaces will have reflections.

Making reflections can be as easy as simply flipping an object vertically and lowering the opacity. But it can also be much more complex, if the object in question is photographed from an angle. We'll show how to split an object into its constituent planes in order to reflect each one individually.

We'll also look at making rippled reflections in water, show how to place people and things inside bottles, and look at that most easy and powerful tool for making instant liquid – Plastic Wrap.

Upon reflection

ADDING A REFLECTION TO A SURFACE converts it from being flat and matt to bright and glossy. The more vivid the reflection is, the shinier the surface appears. Different materials produce varying levels of reflectivity depending on how much light they absorb or let through. A piece of glass on its own will let most of the light through. This results in a sharp but faint reflection. Add a backing to it, such as silver, and you have a mirror. This bounces most of the light back giving a perfect copy of the person or object.

In the following tutorial we'll create a soft reflection by fading it out as it extends further away from the original object. This gives us a similar appearance to the acrylic surfaces used in product photography. This can easily be adjusted to suit your requirements by altering the depth and intensity of the effect.

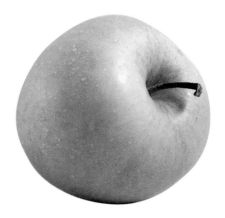

1 Here's our subject. It's already on its own layer. We'll need to duplicate this to use as our reflection. Press *ctrl J*. We'll be using the lower layer for the reflection. This will allow us to place it behind the original giving the impression of depth and substance.

4 Grab the Gradient tool *G*. Selelect a linear black, white gradient. Click the adjustment layer's mask thumbnail to make it active. Position the cursor at the bottom of the document. Holding *Shift*, click and drag the cursor up. I took it to around a third of the way up the original apple here.

2 Flip the layer vertically via Image > Rotate. Use the Move tool **V** to drag the layer down. Hold *Shift* to constrain the movement vertically. This ensures the two image remain aligned. Leave an overlap so the reflection layer remains slightly behind.

3 We'll use a mask to allow us to fade out the reflection a little. Add a Levels adjustment layer between the background layer and the reflection. Accept the default settings. Click the reflection layer's thumbnail in the Layers palette. Press *ctrl* **G** to create a clipping group.

HOT TIP

You can adjust how the mask affects the reflection without having to recreate the gradient each time. Click the mask's thumbnail to make it active. Open the Brightness/ Contrast dialog. Increasing and decreasing the Brightness changes the opacity. Altering the contrast determines how smoothly the blend becomes. A higher value produces a much harsher transition whilst lowering it gives a much more gradual fading effect.

5 We'll add some blur to the reflection to give it slightly more softness. Click the reflection layer's thumbnail to make it active again. Open the Gaussian Blur filter. You won't need to use a lot for this effect; just enough to knock it out of focus a little.

6 To finish off we'll add a shadow. This is created with another copy of the apple filled with black. See the chapter on Light and Shade for more on the technique. For reflective surfaces such as this the shadow needs to be much lighter than if it were cast on a matt surface.

Complex reflections

ON THE PREVIOUS PAGE we created a reflection for an object that had been photographed head-on; a simple task of flipping the image vertically and placing it beneath the original. Problems start, however, when the photo is taken from an angle; as we can see from the image above. Elements can only work in two dimensions so inverting the image gives undesirable results.

For tricky jobs such as this we need to break the object down into separate layers; these can be distorted individually to produce the correct effect.

1 The first step is to divide the object into separate layers: grab the Polygonal Lasso and make an outline around one side of the box. Press *ctrl* *J* to copy it to a new layer. Now repeat this for the other side remembering to make the original box layer active again, of course.

4 Create a Levels adjustment layer below one of the side layers. Make the layer above active again by clicking its thumbnail, and create a clipping group by pressing *ctrl* *G*. Do the same for the second side of the crate. These will be our masks to fade the reflection away.

2 Go back to the front panel layer and flip it vertically then press *ctrl* *T*. Drag it down and match one of the coresponding corners on the base of the original box. Hold *ctrl* *Shift* and drag the opposite center handle up to skew the panel into position.

3 Repeat the last step to add the side panel. At present we have two boxes on top of each other; a good effect in itself but we need to make it more like a reflection. The first thing to do is drop the opacity: around 30% works well here – do this for both layers.

5 Select the Gradient tool *G* and choose a linear black, white gradient. Make sure you have one of the adjustment layer's masks selected. Click half way along the bottom edge of the panel then drag straight up to the top of the reflection. Again, repeat this for the other panel.

6 Finally, we'll add a shadow to place the crate firmly on the ground. Create a new layer above the backround, use the Polygonal Lasso to draw a selection around bottom of the crate. Fill this with black and blur it slightly and lower the opacity a little.

201

Window reflections

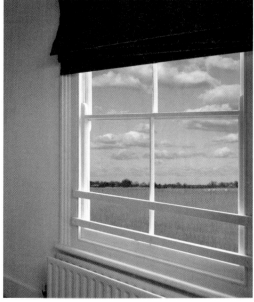

THE VIEW THROUGH THIS WINDOW is far from inspiring: the side of the house next door adds little life to the scene. We'll replace this view with a new one to improve our outlook.

The complications arise when we begin to place figures in the scene. A person in the room will look convincing enough just standing in front of the window, as long as he appears at the right scale for the room; but if we leave it at that, we're ignoring the fact that there should be glass in the window, which should create a reflection.

Adding a reflection certainly makes the glass itself exist as a medium. But how do we make the glass cope with multiple reflections? The answer is to subtract one reflection from the other, to create a wholly convincing effect.

1 We can easily select the window area using the Lasso tool. By making a new layer, filled with a solid color, we create a mask for the window; any view placed on top of this layer, and grouped with it, will be seen 'through' the window.

4 The man is reflecting in the window, and we should be able to see a reflection of the rest of the room as well. Almost any suitable interior will do, as long as its horizontals match that of the window perspective: it doesn't need to be a view of the same room.

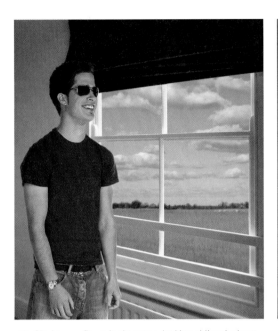

2 Placing our figure in the scene, looking obliquely down the field, adds that human element that brings the image to life. But the window itself looks distinctly empty, and we need to add glass to it.

3 Because of the angle of view – and the symmetry – of our figure, we can simply duplicate him and position a slightly reduced copy (to allow for perspective), grouped with the view, at a low opacity – here, around 50%.

5 The trouble with the previous step was that we could see through the man to the room behind. Of course, his reflection should obscure the room. So hold **ctrl** and click on his thumbnail to load his selection; then switch to the room reflection layer, and delete from there.

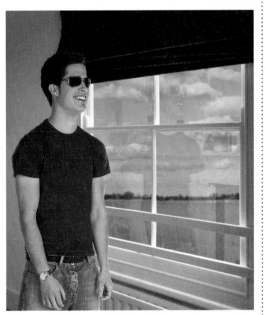

6 We made the reflection of both the room and the man strong enough to see what we were doing in the previous few steps. In reality, we'd expect a much less visible reflection. Here, we've reduced the opacity of both layers to just 20% for a more convincing result.

203

From railway to waterway

CREATING REFLECTIONS IN WATER requires a slightly different approach to those of solid surfaces such as metal or wood. Being a liquid it has different properties to take into account such as turbulence and refraction. We need to distort the reflection to match the state of the water. This could be anything from the subtle ripples on a pond to the hazy elongated lights of cars on a rain-soaked road.

In the following example we'll convert this railway platform into a canal. By using a combination of layers, filters and distortion techniques we can quickly create a realistic water effect which can be tailored to suit many different images, for example: beautiful lakeside scenes, rock pools for a sea life project, or simply puddles on the ground.

1 First we'll create the reflection: draw a selection using the Polygonal Lasso following the perspective of the platform; I've used the yellow letters as a guide. Create the rest of the selection around the top of the image. Now save the selection via the Select menu.

4 Inverse the selection *ctrl* *Shift* *I*. Go to the Select menu and load the selection we saved earlier. Make sure Subtract from Selection is checked and click OK. Now grab the Polygonal Lasso, hold *alt* and remove the area of the platform from the foreground.

7 Use Free Transform to distort the water into place. This doesn't need to be a perfect fit; the texture can become too pixelated if it's stretched too much. We need to adjust enough to stop it looking too flat. Once you've done this, press *ctrl* *G* to group it with the base layer.

2 Copy the selected area to a new layer **ctrl J**. Flip the layer vertically to make a mirror image. Select Image > Transform > Skew: Hold **Shift** and drag the layer down to line the layers up then pull the right-middle handle up to correct the perspective.

3 Hide the reflection layer for now and click the background layer's thumbnail to make it active. Select the line at the edge of the platform with the Magic Wand; hold **Shift** to add any missing areas. Add a small amount of feathering; 1 pixel will be fine here.

5 Create a new layer between thw platform and the reflection. Fill the selection with 50% gray and deselect. Paint in a slight unevenness to the back edge using a hard brush; remember to make it less pronounced as it moves further into the distance.

6 Add another layer above the last. Press **D** to select the default palette, now fill the layer with the Clouds filter to generate a random pattern. Choose the Glass filter from the Distort menu. Set the texture to Frosted, now use the sliders to create a fine rippled effect.

8 Make the reflection layer visible again. Set its blend mode to Soft Light and group it with the water layer. We need to add some ripple to the reflection itself as it would be distorted by the water's surface. This is easily done with the Ocean Ripple filter.

9 Select a large, soft eraser; using the edge, erase some of the lower area of the reflection to fade it out. We'll also add a little tint to the water. We've used a Photo Filter adjustment layer set to cooling at a very low density. You could use a Hue/Saturation adjustment set to colorize.

Goo, slime... and molasses

E LEMENTS IS AWASH WITH FILTERS for performing special effects – everything from knocking up a quick pointillist Seurat painting to making an image look like it's reflected in rippling glass.

Sometimes, though, filters can have surprising results. One of our favorites is Plastic Wrap, which – surprise, surprise – makes objects look as if they're wrapped in plastic. This isn't a job it does very well, but what it can do is to make glistening, slimy liquids from the most basic of ingredients.

Here, we'll show how to use the Plastic Wrap filter to add a few spoons of molasses to the top of this man's head. Why? Well, why not?

1 Begin by making a new layer. Select a mid gray and, using a hard edged brush, paint in the area to be taken up by the goo. If you're having trouble painting convincing drips down the face, try using the Smudge tool to smear the color where you want it to go.

4 Here's the result of that Plastic Wrap filter: a glistening dollop of – well, something gray. We can fix that in the next step. If you find you don't get the effect you want, undo the filter, add a little more shading, and use *ctrl* *F* to apply it again without having to open the dialog.

2 Now add some shading to it using the Dodge and Burn tools, set to Highlights. Remember, if you hold *alt* when using either tool, you'll get the other one temporarily. All we're aiming for here is a random lumpy texture, to give Plastic Wrap something to work on.

3 Choose Filter > Artistic > Plastic Wrap. (Why is it in the Artistic section? No idea.) Push the Highlight Strength and Detail settings up to their maximum – no half measures here – but leave the Smoothness round about the mid point, to add some texture to the stuff.

5 When we change the mode of this layer from Normal to Hard Light, using the pop-up menu at the top of the Layers palette, all the gray disappears, leaving us with just the highlights and shadows. As it stands, this looks more like water than molasses.

6 We can add color using the Hue/Saturation dialog, checking the Colorize button and dragging the Hue slider until we get the color we want. If we left this slider at the far right, we'd get a convincing impression of a bottle of red wine poured over his head. Your choice!

Preserving the occasion

EVER BEEN AT A SPECIAL OCCASION – a birthday, perhaps, or a family event – and wished you could keep it forever? Taking a series of photographs is one method, but here's another that will preserve your favorite memories for all time in a unique way.

The technique we use here will help us to place this girl in a preserving jar. But it could also be used to place snorkeling kids into a fish tank, or to position people and objects in just about any glass container.

We'll begin with the cutout photograph of our girl blowing the candles out on her cake, and then we'll go on to make her look as if she's really inside the glass jar.

1 Here's our bottle. If you want to photograph your own container, make sure it's against a plain white background: a white sheet of paper behind it will work well. And try not to use the flash on your camera, or you'll get an ugly glare off the glass surface.

4 Press *ctrl* **G** to group the new jar layer with the girl's layer, so it only shows up where it overlaps her layer. The rest of the jar is now returned to its original appearance. But the effect is now too strong: the girl has almost disappeared inside that container.

2 When we place the girl on top of the jar, we can resize her to fit the shape using Free Transform (*ctrl* **T**). She may now fit the jar, but the effect is far from convincing: we need to add a couple of treatments to make it look as if she's really inside.

3 Duplicate the jar layer, and move it above the girl's layer; then change the mode of the jar to Hard Light, using the pop-up menu at the top of the Layers palette. The effect is to make the whole jar too bright, and we can correct this in the next step.

5 We can reduce the strength of the effect by lowering the opacity of the duplicated jar layer. Experiment with different settings to see what looks best: here, an opacity of 40% gives a good balance. The value you end up with will depend very much on the glass container you photograph.

6 Finally, we need to pay attention to the thick glass at the top of the jar, where it meets the lid. Use a small, soft-edged Eraser to remove those parts of the girl's head behind these thicker glass areas, and we'll get a much more convincing result.

HOT TIP

Changing the opacity of the duplicated jar in step 5 is the key to making this technique work. Rather than dragging the Opacity slider, there's an easier way. With the Move tool selected, use the number keys, either on the keypad or on the top row of the keyboard. Pressing 4 will give you 40% opacity, 5 will give 50%, up to 0 to return to 100%. You can get intermediate values by pressing two keys in quick succession – so pressing 4 then 5 will give you 45%.

209

Keeping it real

POSSIBLY THE GREATEST COMPLIMENT you can receive for one of your montages is when the viewer does not realize it is one in the first place. This need not be as time consuming and laborious as you may think: a large part of producing a convincing image, after all, is creating an illusion to fool the viewer: it may not survive close scrutiny, but unless we're trying to conclusively prove to NASA that we had reached the Moon long before Neil Armstrong, we can afford a little artistic license.

Creating a realistic image depends on a number of factors, most importantly the individual components of the artwork need to fit together as seamlessly as possible: the direction at which the people and objects are lit needs to be the same – there's no point having someone caught in a spotlight, for instance, if their face still appears to be in shadow. We also need to make sure the shadows themselves are correct and, more importantly, present to begin with; everything casts a shadow of some sort, even if they are too faint to notice initially — they help to define depth, placing their associated object within its surroundings. Getting the color right also plays an essential role: be careful not to use garish hues as this could result in an unnatural looking image.

So with all that said, how do we go about translating it into our artwork? The answer is often staring right back at us: a lot of the time we'll be adding to an existing photo so we can take our cues from there, adjusting the new elements accordingly; sampling the colors and tones, comparing them as we go. Things become trickier when it comes to building a picture from the ground up where our clues aren't there to guide us — we're far from helpless though.

Just as a traditional artist studies their subject and surroundings to set it to canvas, we can do the same. It's by no means a crime to use reference material to make sure we achieve the correct effect and it's certainly preferential to trying to use guesswork alone. A good starting point is, of course, the internet, and image search engines such as Google or Yahoo are superb resources; it's highly probable that we'll find what we're looking for, and, because we're not actually including the image within our artwork, copyright is not an issue and we need not be too concerned with its dimensions as long as it's possible to see the detail. We can, of course, take our own reference shots as well: again, these don't need to be award-winning photographs, they just need to be of a good enough quality to see the effect, so even quick snaps from a cell phone should be sufficient.

There will be occasions when we need to see different versions of the same effect and also have the ability to view it from different angles; something that a still image cannot offer. In these situations improvising with props is often a great solution, they don't necessarily need to be the exact objects, and only need to be crudely put together, as long as the outcome is a good representation, we can transpose it to our design. It's surprising how many things we can find within immediate reach with which we can improvise: we might, for example, want to see how a shadow falls across an uneven surface such as a staircase; so instead of grabbing the nearest family member and have them stand in different positions, we can quickly put together an impromptu mock-up by folding a sheet of paper and positioning a suitably illustrative object; then use a flashlight or similar maneuverable light source to create the desired effect.

We're not always going to be producing images depicting plain old reality, of course, we'll often be creating montages that are highly stylized or in a fantasy theme: there will always be a demand for fairy princesses and other such magical pictures, after all. This often demands more attention to detail than with their more sublime counterparts; people tend to scrutinise them far more closely, even though they know they cannot be real. It's highly unlikely we'll stumble across a real photo in a search but we can still apply the same principles from the real world to our artwork: reflections, shadows and color still play their part in creating a convincing scene. We do have the advantage that nobody can really say how a picture of this ilk really should look, so we can be a little more lenient with the rules.

Finally, remember that there will always be flaws and unexpected elements in a real scene: try not to make your images too clinical. Try adding some random areas of light and shadow — it's often the smallest details that have the most impact.

■ Two images of a car on an airport runway. It's the identical car in both photographs; but in the top image it looks false and out of place, whereas in the bottom one it belongs in the scene. The difference is that in the top picture the car is too high for the perspective of the scene; in the bottom one, the perspective is correct.

212

11
The third dimension

ALMOST EVERY PHOTOGRAPH WE TAKE captures a scene in three dimensions. When we want to add, edit or adjust objects in the scene, we need to pay close attention to the perspective in the original scene if we're going to achieve anything like a convincing montage.

There are complex rules governing how perspective works, and these have been refined ever since they were first formulated by the Persian philosopher Alhazen in the 11th century. Since we're dealing with photographed images, rather than a blank canvas, we can read the existing perspective out of the scene: in this way, by using our eye and drawing vanishing point lines, we can guarantee that any new picture elements we add are consistent with the scene we started with.

Lifting the lid

DESPITE THE HUGE AMOUNT OF IMAGES available through stock photography sites, there will come a time where you cannot find exactly the right one for your project. This is not always a problem as we'll see in the following tutorial.

The image of the wooden box is perfect except it's closed, and we want it open. Unlike the real thing we cannot simply remove its lid: the rear sides of the box don't exist. With a few selections and transformations we'll create the missing areas using copies of the remaining sections.

1 Our first task is to isolate the lid from the rest of the box. The Polygonal Lasso **L** is perfect for this. Create a selection around the whole of the lid. Press **ctrl** **Shift** **J** to cut it away from the rest of the image. Hiding the layer shows the problem: we only have half a box.

4 Make sure the box layer is active. Create a selection around the front side of the box. Press **ctrl** **J** to create a copy. Move this layer down the stack so it's behind the rest. Now reposition and distort it into place as the back side of the box.

2 Make the lid visible again. Change the layer order so the lid is behind the box. Enter Free Transform *ctrl* *T*. Start by lowering the lid so its front corner lines up with the existing sides of the box. Hold *ctrl*. Now distort the outer corners to match.

3 Next we'll cut a hole in the top. This serves two purposes: we can use the edges as a guide for the missing sides. It will also give them substance. Create a selection following the perimeter of the lid but a few pixels inside the edge. Press *Backspace*.

It can be helpful to have a guide to follow when distorting in perspective. Sometimes you'll be able to use other areas of the original image. You can also create your own reference. This could form part of the object, as with the rim of the box. You can also use layers to create an overlay which can be turned on and off during the creation process.

5 Repeat the last step to create the remaining side; remember to switch back to the box layer first. Switch to the back side layer. Make another copy. Again, move it to the bottom of the layer stack. Distort this to create the floor of the box.

6 All that remains is to add some shading inside the box. Grab the Burn tool *O*. Set the mode to Highlights. Use a large soft brush to paint in some shadows; you'll need to switch between the layers. We only need a few subtle areas in this instance as the original lighting works quite well.

Lifting the lid 2

ON THE PRECEDING PAGE we opened a box by removing its lid completely. You may, however, decide that you want to keep it in the image, opening as though it were hinged.

This is not difficult to achieve. We can't, of course, simply pivot the lid to open it. This is two-dimensional artwork after all. Instead we'll use geometry in our favor. By flipping and rotating the lid, its angle is mirrored against the box. Once in place we can use a variation on the previous technique to create the hollowed out effect.

1 To avoid unecessary steps in creating the open box we'll use the completed image from the last technique. The original lid has been selected and placed on a separate layer. The first thing to do is flip the layer. Do this by selecting Flip Layer Vertically under Image > Rotate.

4 Use the Move tool **V** to push the panel toward the rear of the lid. This creates a recessed area. Don't place it too far back, we need to give the illusion that it has thickness. Again we can see the problem. The rear and side panels are missing.

HOT TIP

Whilst this is a
very efficient
method of
opening a
lid, your
composition
may require it
at a different
angle. To do this
you'll first need
to break the
lid down into
separate layers
comprising its
component
parts. These can
be manouvered
into the
correct position
individually
to produce
the desired
effect. A similar
technique is
used to create
a complex
reflection in the
chapter on shiny
surfaces.

2 Use free transform to move and rotate the lid into place at the rear of the box. You'll notice it doesn't quite fit: it's too wide. Use the corner handles to squash the lid up a little so it meets the corners of the box. Make sure it meets the edge; you may need to rotate it a little more.

3 We could leave it at this stage. That lid looks a little heavy, though. Use the Polygonal lasso to create a selection a few pixels within the edge of the lid's panel. Press *ctrl* *Shift* *J* to remove the area and place it on its own layer. Drop it behind the lid in the Layers palette.

5 Click the lid layer's thumbnail to make it active. Select the top edge of the lid. Press *ctrl* *J* to copy it to a new layer. Drop this new layer behind the lid and panel layers in the stack. Use free transform to distort it into position. Repeat to create the missing right-hand side panel.

6 Select the Burn tool *O*. Set the mode to Highlights. Choose a large soft edged tip. Paint in some areas of shadow on the inside of the lid; particularly at the top and in the corners where less light would reach. You may also want to darken the inside of the box itself.

217

Tiling the floor

THERE'S NOTHING LIKE A SPOT of
redecorating to brighten things up. The
old wooden floor of the changing room in this
photo could certainly do with renwewing. Let's
replace it with something a little more lavish: a
nice marble checker to complement the border
on the wall, perhaps?

The effect is not as difficult to produce as it
might seem. We'll create the pattern on a layer;
using the Clouds filter to add the marbling
effect. We already have the existing perspective
to use as a guide so it's simply a matter of
distorting the new floor into position.

You can, of course, use any pattern or
texture with this technique. Perhaps use it to
visualize ideas for decorating your room before
you commit to a particular design.

1 Create a new layer. Select the rectangular marquee **M**.
Draw a selection holding **Shift** to keep it square. Fill this
black. Holding **ctrl** **alt**, click and drag the selection to create
a copy. Place it along side the last square. Fill this with
white. Repeat this twice more to finish the pattern.

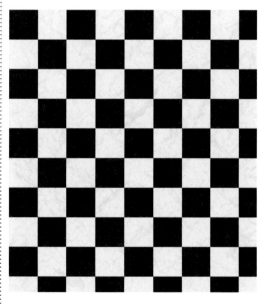

4 Add another new layer. Fill this with the Clouds filter.
Apply the Find Edges filter from the Stylize menu. This
gives us a nice marble like texture. Set the Blend Mode to
Difference. Lower the opacity slightly to reduce the contrast.
Press **ctrl** **E** to merge the layers together.

2 We'll use this to create a repeating pattern. Load the layer's selection. Select Define Pattern from Selection from the Edit menu. Give it a meaningful name for later reference and click OK. At this stage you can either delete the layer or hide it as it's no longer needed.

3 Create a new layer at the top of the stack. Press **Shift** **Backspace** to open the Fill dialog. Choose Pattern for the Contents from the drop-down menu. Select the tile pattern from the palette. Clicking OK will fill the whole layer with our new pattern.

5 Now we have our new floor we need to distort it into position. Enter Free Transform. Hold **ctrl** and distort the corner points to match the floor in the photo. You'll need to zoom out to be able to manoeuvre the left-hand side of the new floor into position.

6 We need to mask out the areas around the bench and the cubicles. This can be achieved by using the original floor as a clipping mask (see Chapter 3). A Hue/Saturation adjustment adds a slight color cast and darkens the floor down. Some shading is added to complete the effect.

HOT TIP

It can be tricky to get the perspective right when you don't have the whole area to match up to. Try to find as many points of reference as possible. In this image we have the lines of the original floor. The problem is they are hidden beneath the new layer. You can, of course, lower the opacity; a better solution here, however, is to change the tile layer's blend mode to Multiply or Screen. This will hide the white or black squares respectively allowing us to accurately match up the visible edges.

219

Opening doors

1 Use the Polygonal Lasso tool to trace the shape of the door, then use *ctrl* *J* to make a new layer from it. Load the door region by *ctrl*-clicking on its thumbnail, then make a new layer behind it, filled with black. The three layers are shown here offset to show the stacking order.

ONE OF THE NEATEST TRICKS we can play in Elements is to open a closed door. It's impressive to see it done, but here's the real trick: it's very easy to do.

The procedure makes use of the Free Transform tool, which performs perspective distortions with ease – and without us even asking anything of it. Distort a corner handle or two, and the object in question will do its best to fill the space in a true three-dimensional manner.

In this tutorial we'll concentrate on opening the door and giving it some thickness so it looks real. The view through the door we'll leave as a gaping black hole; overleaf, we'll see how to fill this hole with a convincing view.

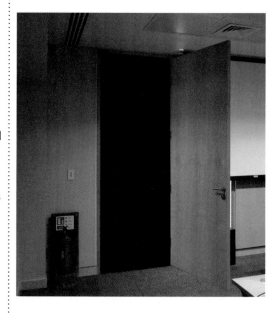

5 We can distort this new piece of door in a similar way to how we distorted the door itself, using Free Transform to adjust not only the width, but the height. The edge where the side touches the door should be slightly higher than the edge away from the door.

2 Enter Free Transform on the door layer using *ctrl* *T*, and drag the center left handle to the right in order to flip the door so it's facing the other way.

3 Now for some perspective. Hold *ctrl* *Shift* as you drag the top right corner handle up; repeat this for the bottom right handle, until the door looks like it fits the space.

4 To give the door some thickness, we'll need to add a side. Make a rectangular selection with the Marquee tool from the door itself, and make a new layer from it; move it to the side.

HOT TIP

Getting the perspective on the open door exactly right is the only tricky part of this exercise. There's no simple way to describe precisely how this should be done: but if it looks right, then it probably is. In step 5, we distort the side of the door to match the opened door. It can be hard to do this accurately in Free Transform, so here's a simple solution: make the side higher than you need, then remove the top and bottom with the Lasso or even a hard-edged Eraser to fit the door.

6 Brighten up this door side a little, using Levels or the Brightness/Contrast adjustment – whichever you prefer. Here, we've also drawn in a lock mechanism, just for the sake of completeness: a rectangular selection was filled with a color sampled from the door handle.

7 Now, that all-important shadow. It's only a tiny amount of shadow, painted on a new layer beneath the door layer, but it makes all the difference to the realism of the scene. And how about copying the original room, grouped with the black layer, to make the view through the door?

221

Using perspective

PERPSECTIVE IS ONE of the trickiest techniques to master in Elements. It's the factor that distinguishes convincing montages from those that just don't feel quite right. But by following a few straightforward rules, it's possible to make perspective work for you, rather than against you.

The key to reading perspective in a photograph lies in using horizontal lines in the original image to calculate where the vanishing point of the image lies: once we've established this, anything we draw will naturally fit the scene.

1 In this photograph of an office hallway, we're going to remove the elevator and replace it with a corridor. At first glance, the task looks daunting. While there are plenty of horizontals here that are parallel to the wall facing us, there are very few at right angles to it. But we're fortunate in having that side wall, containing the doors, just in view: using these, we can read the perspective for the scene, which is enough to give us our vanishing point.

3 We can now draw two new perspective lines, to give us the top and bottom of our hallway. Start from the left corners, and finish at the vanishing point. It's now possible to draw our first wall, by using the Polygonal Lasso tool to follow these persepective lines, then filling the selection with a color to match the other walls. Group this wall layer with the black base layer we made in the previous step, so it only shows up where the two overlap.

4 We can now recolor the black layer to make a suitably colored ceiling. It's behind the wall layer, so the wall still shows up. To make the carpet, copy a section of the existing carpet and paste it in place, grouped with the ceiling layer but behind the wall layer. You may need to distort it to fit.

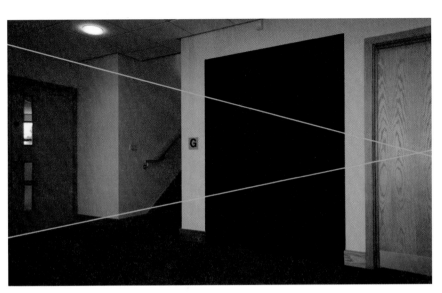

2 We'll begin by making a new layer. Then choose the Shapes tool, set to draw straight lines. Draw two lines that follow the strongest horizontals in the left-hand wall: in this case, the bottom of the doors, and the very top of the wall. Where these lines converge, over on the far right of the image, is the vanishing point. Next, on another layer, draw a selection that matches the face of the elevator opening – going right down to floor level – and fill this with black.

5 After drawing in the end wall, finishing off the scene is simply a matter of copying the elements we want from elsewhere in the picture. Here, we've taken a copy of the door on the far left, and distorted it to match the perspective of the hallway.

A section of skirting board, taken from the far left of the facing wall, is copied and then stretched to run along the base of the new wall, and another small copy bent around the end wall. Finally, we made a new layer and added some shading to it with a large, soft-edged brush, to give the impression of the corridor darkening as it recedes into the distance. This final touch accentuates the sense of the corridor as a real space, adding extra realism to the scene.

HOT TIP

When we distort the copies of the original door in step 5, we run into a tiny problem: because the door wasn't viewed head on, we can't use the bounding box in Free Transform to match the perspective of the view. Instead, adjust the distortion so that the bottom of the door lines up with the bottom of the wall, then drag the top corner so that it follows the angle of the top of the wall, once again pointing directly towards the vanishing point.

Make your own jigsaws

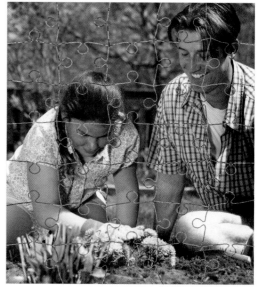

WITH ALL THE MULTITUDE OF FILTERS in Elements, it's perhaps surprising that, hidden among the Stained Glass and other effects, there isn't one for creating jigsaws.

Here's a technique that makes use of a custom Shape that we've included for you on the CD. To install it, follow these steps:

1. Exit Photoshop Elements.

2. Locate the file Cheat.csh in the Goodies folder on the CD.

3. Copy the Cheat.csh file to the folder Program Files\Adobe Photoshop Elements 6.0\Presets on your hard drive.

4. Restart Photoshop Elements.

The jigsaw shape will appear in the Shapes sub-menu when you switch to the Shapes tool, in the item named Cheat.

1 Choose the shape Jigsaw Portrait from the Cheat section of the Shapes dialog. Once the shape is selected, use the Shapes tool to drag from corner to corner within your image, so that the entire space is filled with the jigsaw pattern. You'll see it appear as faint lines as you do so.

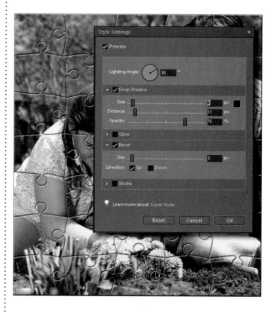

4 To give the pieces some depth, add an Emboss effect. Open the Style Settings dialog and reduce the size of the Emboss to about 5 pixels; add a slight drop shadow to make the pieces look more three-dimensional. You can play around with the Emboss settings until it looks right.

2 Once you release the mouse button, the Shapes layer will be filled with the default color – generally blue. We'll only be using this as a template, so there's no need to change the color of the layer: it won't appear in the final illustration.

3 Load up the Shapes layer's pixel area by holding **ctrl** and clicking on its thumbnail in the Layers palette. Then return to the image layer, and use **ctrl J** to make a new layer from that selection. Hide the Shapes layer to see the image made up of jigsaw pieces.

HOT TIP

We've included two versions of the jigsaw on the CD – one in portrait (vertical) orientation, the other in a landscape (horizontal) shape. Choose whichever one is most appropriate for the shape of the image you're working on.

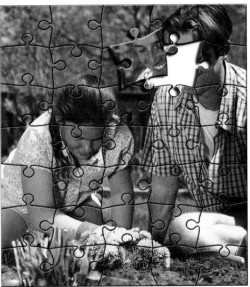

5 Now let's make the dividing lines clearer. Load up the selection of the Shapes layer again, then inverse the selection using **ctrl Shift I**; now everything except the pieces is selected. Make a new layer, and fill the selection with black to make the lines between the pieces.

6 To take one piece out of the jigsaw, go to the lines layer we just created and click in one of the pieces with the Magic Wand tool. Now return to the image layer, and use **ctrl Shift J** to cut that selection to a new layer. Move it to the top of the layer stack, and move and rotate it as you like.

Out of bounds

1 Here's our original painting. The format – one girl helping another down from a wall – is perfect for our purposes.

2 The first step is to select and copy the figures to a new layer, using a combination of your favorite selection tools.

THE 'OUT OF BOUNDS' TECHNIQUE is a popular one with Elements artists, and it's not hard to see why: breaking a picture out of its frame makes for an arresting image. That's why we used the technique on the cover of this book.

The process can be as simple or as complex as you want to make it. Here, we'll look at a rather more detailed version of the trick, using not a photograph, but a painting – *Little Thieves* or *Petites Maraudeuses*, by William-Adolphe Bougeuereau.

6 The carpet is added on a new layer: solid color, Gaussian Noise, then Gaussian Blur. We've also deleted the section of wall behind the painting.

7 Use Shadows/Highlights to brighten that dark skirt, and the Dodge tool to lighten the legs; then clone out the foliage on the skirt.

3 Now place the picture frame between the two layers, distorting it using Free Transform until it follows the angle of the wall in the painting.

4 Let's now add our own wall. Make a rectangular selection on a new layer filled with solid color; the skirting board is easily painted at the bottom.

5 Now enter Free Transform and, holding *ctrl* *Shift*, drag the bottom right corner down until it matches the painting's perspective.

The real key to this technique lies in constructing a setting to match the perspective of the original painting or photograph. You'll almost certainly have to adjust the lighting, particularly in the shadow areas: here, the feet looked fine in the original painting, but were much too dark against the carpet.

8 The shadows behind the girls give them some distance from the wall: use the techniques outlined in Chapter 5.

9 We've added a chair to give a sense of the room continuing out of the frame, and to make that plain wall look a little less bare.

10 Finally, add shadows for the chair and picture frame. And while we're at it, we may as well include a plaque to the painter.

RGB or CMYK?

PICTURE THE SCENE: you've spent hours creating the perfect birthday card in Elements. It features a lovingly crafted cutout image against a bright green background, a dazzlingly bright red headline, and a contrasting blue caption. But when you print it out on your inkjet printer, the text looks dull and lifeless, and the background is far darker than it looked on the screen – despite having used the best quality glossy photo paper. What can have gone wrong?

The problem is the fundamental difference between what you see on the screen and what can be printed on paper. And it all comes down to two acronyms, RGB and CMYK.

RGB stands for red, green and blue, and refers to the colors used by computer monitors. In standard 8-bit mode, each pixel on your screen can display each of these three colors in 256 different levels of brightness. 256 is 2^8, or 2 multiplied by itself 8 times – which is what 8-bit means. By combining these three basic colors, each pixel can display 2^8 x 2^8 x 2^8 different colors – over 16 million in total.

We start with a black screen, and the more color we throw on it, the brighter it becomes. These are known as 'additive' colors for this reason: we're adding light to blackness. When we add the maximum value of each of the three primary colors, we get white.

Printing ink on paper, however, works in precisely the opposite way. Rather than using red, green and blue, printers use cyan, magenta and yellow. But when we print, we start off with white paper; the more colors we add, the darker the result (just as you find when you mix paints together). These are known as 'subtractive' colors. If we add 100% of cyan, magenta and yellow together, we get black. Or rather, we don't; we get a muddy brown. That's why printers use an additional color, black, to deepen the shadows and strengthen the printed image. The four colors combined give us CMYK. Surprisingly, no-one seems to know precisely what the 'K' stands for. Most claim it means 'key', although that seems a poor substitute for 'black'.

When you mix the primary colors together, either on screen or on paper, you get some surprising results. On screen, mixing red and green makes yellow; red and blue make magenta; and green and blue make cyan. Do those colors sound familiar? They should do – they're the primary colors of printing inks. And, when printing, mixing magenta and yellow produces red, magenta and cyan makes blue, and yellow and cyan makes green.

So what does this have to do with poor quality printing? The trouble is that while your monitor is capable of displaying a huge range of colors, CMYK is capable of reproducing only a very limited part of that color 'gamut', as it's known. That's the reason why commercial printers use additional Pantone colors, chosen from swatch books similar to those you'd use to choose household paints. If you want a color that can't be achieved with CMYK, you need to use additional inks.

Some inkjet printers try to get around this problem by using six colors, rather than four. And this does expand the range slightly, but the unfortunate fact remains that not everything you see on your monitor is capable of being reproduced on paper.

What's the solution, then? Can't we just convert our images to CMYK before we print them, and see what the difference is? Not in Elements, we can't, although we can in its big brother Photoshop. The ability to prepare print-ready artwork is one of the reasons Photoshop costs nearly ten times as much.

Avoid 100% green or blue, as these are the colors least likely to reproduce well; dazzling pinks are also problematic, although 100% magenta and solid red will work well. If a color combination on your monitor looks larger than life, then that's probably a good indication that you won't be able to print it. Ultimately, though, it comes down to experience: seasoned users get to know which colors will work, and which won't. If in doubt, sample colors from your photographs rather than creating them from the color picker – you're much more likely to get printable colors that way.

■ Two versions of the same vacation scene. The top one, as a Photoshop Elements file, takes up just over 4Mb of disk space. The one on the right, saved as a low quality JPEG file, takes up just 78K. Can't spot the difference? That's because Elements' innovative Save for Web feature can make huge size savings with minimal loss of quality.

12

Print and the internet

CREATING FANTASTIC IMAGES in Elements is one thing. Getting it off your computer screen is another matter entirely. As with most techniques, there are right and wrong ways of doing the job.

In this chapter we'll explain how to save files for speedy internet delivery, both for single images and for animations. (We'll also look at how to create eye-catching animations directly in Elements.)

We'll also show a useful technique for making your printed results look far more like what you see on screen, without having to get your printer or monitor calibrated. And we'll walk through the processes involved in designing the cover of this book in Elements.

Saving files for the internet

W E ALL WANT to share our photographs and montages with others, and the internet provides a simple, easy way to do just that. But rather than just taking your Elements file and uploading it to a website, you first need to save it in a format that web browsers will understand.

JPEG, GIF and PNG are the three most common file types. Elements provides a useful way to save images for web delivery: it's called Save for Web, and you'll find it under the File menu.

Here, we'll look at what each of the three formats has to offer, and see how to use the Save for Web dialog to get the best possible results from your digital images.

1 Here's a detail of our original photograph, enlarged so we can see the detail – but at 313K, it's far too big for internet delivery.

2 As a 256-color GIF image, we can see a little blockiness appearing in the white of the teeth: this image is a hefty 264K in size.

3 Reducing the number of colors in this GIF file to 64 reduces the file size to 168K, but we can clearly see the 'dither pattern' in the skin tones.

4 As an 8 color GIF, the file size comes down to 72K: it's now acquired the appearance of a poorly photocopied sepia print.

5 As a JPEG file with a quality of 50, this is very close to the original, but its size has been reduced to just 73K – fine for the internet.

6 Taking the JPEG quality down to 20 produces some marked 'blockiness', and reduces the file size to 38K.

7 For the sake of comparison, here's the file at a JPEG setting of 0. The image is just about unusable, but takes up just 19K of space.

8 A 24-bit PNG file produces the best results, but at a cost: this file is a massive 604K – nearly twice the size of the original.

The first step in Save for Web is to choose the file type. JPEG is best for photographs; GIF is best for areas with a lot of flat color, such as buttons and badges. PNG supports transparency, unlike JPEGs, and produces good quality – but at the cost of increased file size.

Unless you're creating page furniture for web pages, it's best to stick to JPEG format, as this will give you the best results. There's a trade-off between file size and quality: the better the quality, the larger the file will be, so the longer it will take people to download.

A JPEG setting of 50 or more will produce an image that's almost indistinguishable from the original file. The more complex an image, the larger the file will be: so a shot of a cloudy sky will produce a much larger file if there's an intricate fence in front of it.

As you drag the Quality slider, you can see the results of the JPEG compression in the right-hand pane (the left one always shows the original

image). If it's not showing an area you want to concentrate on, drag within the window to move it and both images will pan together. You can also zoom in using the Magnifying Glass tool at the top left to see an area of interest in detail.

JPEG files can be set to 'progressive', which means that they will load in stages, each pass producing a more detailed version of the image. This was an issue when most people had slow modems, but is now rarely used.

Beneath each image is a readout showing the file type, the size the resulting file will be, and the time taken to download it. Click the tiny arrow at the top right of the images to change the speed of download: the default 28K applies to old-fashioned modems, which are hardly relevant in the era of high speed broadband.

You can also choose to reduce the physical image size as well, using the New Size section (center right). This will, of course, reduce the file size as

well, but you need to be sure of the dimensions you want to end up with before playing with these numbers.

If you have a favorite combination that works well for your images, you can save it as a preset, and then apply it to each image that passes through the Save for Web dialog. You can also choose to include ICC profiles, which aim to maintain consistent color: unless your computer has been calibrated to do this, it's best avoided.

The Matte box is used for saving GIF and PNG images with transparency: if you want to place images on a colored background in a web page, specify that color here and the transparent pixels will be blended with it. This is necessary because GIFs and 8-bit PNG files only support one level of transparency – on or off.

When you've chosen your settings, press OK and the standard file Save dialog will open. Be sure to specify a different name for your file to avoid overwriting the existing image.

233

Animated GIFs

MOVEMENT IS ONE of the characteristics that most distinguishes the internet from printed books. We can create short animations right inside Elements, using the Save for Web feature.

In this example, we've made a simple montage containing just five layers: the background, with the road and sky; the clouds; the car; the crate on the back of the car; and the shadow beneath it.

By moving each of these layers around and making a new composite copy as a separate layer, we can create our animation as a series of separate Elements layers. It's then an easy matter to string these together to make a moving image.

We can't show our finished animation in this book, of course, but it is on the CD if you want to see how it looks when it's moving.

1 Begin with Select All (*ctrl* *A*) then by Merged Copy (*ctrl* *Shift* *C*). This makes a copy of everything in the artwork. Now choose Paste (*ctrl* *V*) and move that copy to the top of the pile, as shown in the Layers palette (right).

4 The same process once more: move the clouds and jiggle the car and the crate, then Select All, Merged Copy, and Paste. Remember to hide the previous composite copy by clicking its 'eye' icon in the Layers palette before you attempt to move anything. When moving the clouds, hold the *Shift* key to make sure you're moving them horizontally.

5 When we get the big cloud over to the far left (frame 4 in our animation), we now need to make a copy of this cloud layer and drag it over to the right, so the small cloud is just creeping in from that side. This will allow us to make the animation run for ever.

6 For frame 5 and for subsequent frames, we need to move both the original clouds layer and its copy. In Elements 5 and later you can select both layers together in the Layers palette; but it's just as easy to use *ctrl* *E* to merge the two layers together, so you can move them as one.

7 You can make as many frames as you like in your animation: we're using just six. In this final frame, the small cloud, which has been sliding in from the right, is now approaching its original position, and we can see the copy of the big cloud starting to make an appearance too. By duplicating the cloud layers in this way we're able to create an animation which appears to run seamlessly for ever.

2 That's frame 1 done. To make frame 2, first hide the first merged copy, then drag the clouds layer to the left a little way. Move the car up a fraction, and rotate the crate to give the impression of them jiggling around as they move.

3 Now repeat the Select All, Merged Copy, Paste procedure as before, to create another new layer – and, once again, make sure it's at the top of the layer stack. Each of these new composite layers will form a single frame in our animation. Here's how the Layers palette will look after the second frame is complete.

HOT TIP

Although we've gone to some lengths to wrap the background clouds around so that the animation will loop convincingly, you don't need to do this with every animation. However you choose to animate your constructions, do be sure to save a copy before deleting all the original layers: Elements can only work with one layer equalling one frame of animation, and you don't want to accidentally lose all your hard work.

8 Here's how your Layers palette will look after all six frames have been completed. We now need to delete all the original layers – including the background – leaving just the six composite frames of the animation.

9 Now's a good time to save your document. But rather than overwriting the original, choose Save As and give it a different name: we don't want to lose all those individual layers that we've had to delete in the previous step.

Choose File > Save for Web to open the dialog, which will look exactly as it did on the previous pages. This time, though, check the Animate box near the top of the dialog window.

The number of frames in the animation is set by the number of layers in the document – one for each layer. But we can specify the time each frame is to last for, as well as whether the animation will run just once or will loop forever. This is the option we'll choose here: that's why we wrapped the clouds around in that way.

Adjust the Dither and number of colors, if you like, to reduce the size of the file; our example weighs in at over 600K, larger than a standard web animation would normally be.

Click the Preview button at the bottom to see how your animation will look in a browser: this is the first time you'll be able to see it moving. When you're happy with the timing, press OK to save the animation as a GIF file.

Easy print matching

WITH COMPUTERS GETTING EASIER and easier to use, it's something of an irony that the biggest stumbling block seems to be when we revert to older technology – and that's in getting our images onto paper.

There's no real substitute for having your printer properly calibrated, perhaps investing in a monitor calibration device as well. But many of us don't have the money, the time or the inclination to get this involved in our printing.

Instead, here's a simple workaround that may help to fool your printer into producing results that more closely match the image you see on your monitor. It's not 100% guaranteed, but the chances are it will fix a lot of print problems.

1 Here's the problem. You've downloaded your photos to your computer, and you've adjusted them in Elements so that they look their best. But when you print them out, the results look quite different to what you see on screen: the prints may be darker, they may have a strong color cast, and so on.

3 Back in the original file, make a new Levels adjustment layer. With this one, adjust the image – as seen through the first adjustment – to make your image look as close as possible to the original. By doing this, we're (hopefully) reversing the process of color change produced by the printer.

2 With the image you've just printed open in Elements, make a new Levels adjustment layer. Tweak the Levels settings to make the image on screen match the printout as closely as possible. What we're doing here is to simulate the color shift your printer will have upon the image, so we can compensate for it.

4 Now hide the original adjustment layer, leaving just the second. The idea is that by then printing this file, the printer will produce the same color shift it did before; and as we saw from the original adjustment layer, this should produce a print that's far closer to your original photograph.

5 Save your second adjustment layer by dragging it into a new, empty file. When you next print, drag it into the document for improved results.

HOT TIP

You may find this technique produces too strong an effect, with a print that's skewed the other way. If so, try lowering the opacity of the adjustment layer until you get a result that works.

Once you're happy with the result, you can drag this second adjustment layer into any of your images before printing, and it should help to compensate for the misdoings of your printer.

The cover of this book

BOOK COVERS ARE ABOUT the most challenging design process for any Elements artist. They have to be arresting and eye-catching, and above all have to be a good advertisement for the book. We decided to use an Out of Bounds image to show off the full capabilities of Elements.

After much deliberation – our original rough had a dolphin leaping out of the screen, then a dog and a horse – we settled on a boy reaching for a tool from the Elements toolbox. Elements users, our marketing department insisted, tended to have children more than dolphins.

This cover includes examples of several of the tutorials in the book, to give an idea of the scope and range of techniques that the book would cover.

We started with a simple cutout of a laptop to form the basis for our montage.

1 To make the tray, we began by drawing a flat gray shape on a new layer (top). We added shading to this (middle) using Dodge and Burn, masking out the base to get a hard edge in there. All the Elements tools were then added and grouped with this tray layer so it appeared that they fit inside it.

4 We selected the boy's head and arm, and copied these to a new layer. We then moved the original boy layer behind the interface layer, so it appeared to be viewed through the screen; we also erased the boy's thumb and fingers to go behind the brush and magnifying glass.

2 We took a screenshot of the Elements interface, and modified it to show a couple of examples of tutorials from the book. After deleting the image area, we then distorted this screenshot using Free Transform to fit the shape of the laptop screen.

3 The photograph of the boy was placed on top so that his head was sticking out of the top of the screen, and his arm reaching to pick up one of the tools in the box. Again, we used Free Transform to scale and rotate him until he appeared in the correct position.

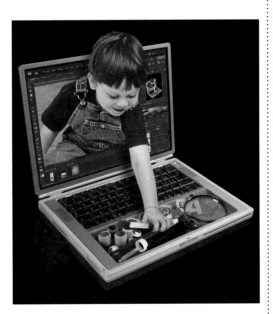

5 After placing a new background behind the boy, within the screen area, we painted soft shadows on a new layer behind the boy's head, and beneath his arm. These accentuate the sense of him reaching out of the screen, adding a greater feeling of realism.

6 Finally, we changed the background color to black, and duplicated the edge of the laptop, the lid and the interface. We moved these layers to the back of the composition, distorting them to fit and lowering their opacity to 30% to make the reflection.

Glossary

Actual size
Displaying the image on screen so that one pixel in the image exactly matches one pixel on the monitor. This is not the same as print size, which is determined by the resolution of the image.

Adjustment layer
Special layers that perform non-destructive tonal and color adjustments to all or part of the artwork; they can be turned on and off and altered as required.

Aliasing
The opposite of anti-aliasing: no attempt is made at blending elements of the artwork to avoid jagged edges. This does have its uses: it can be used with very small fonts to avoid them becoming unreadable.

Alignment
A set of tools on the Options bar to force multiple layers to line up with each other using edges or centers.

Alpha channel
An area used to store a layer's selection information. This can be loaded and saved whilst the document is open; some file types can store alpha channels permanently with the image information.

Anti-aliasing
The method of creating a smooth transition between contrasting colors to avoid harsh jagged lines.

Background layer
By default, this is the base layer upon which all others are added. Most operations can be performed on this apart from moving and applying styles.

Bitmap
The method of creating an image by adding individual pixels of a specific color in a two-dimensional grid. Most images produced in Elements use this process.

Blend Mode
Used to combine the content of two or more layers by blending the upper layer with the layer beneath in different ways to produce a variety of effects.

Brightness/contrast
An adjustment method used for enhancing the strength of layers and images.

Channel
The area that holds the color information of an image. In Elements there are three channels; red, green and blue that are mixed together in varying amounts to define all the colors.

Clipping Group
Hiding areas of the artwork by grouping two or more layers: the base layer acts as a mask template, its pixels defining what is visible on the layers above.

CMYK
Abbreviation for Cyan, Magenta, Yellow and Black – the colors used for reproducing images in printed materials.

Color settings
A section of Elements' Preferences that set whether images are displayed for on-screen viewing or optimized for printing.

Compression
The method of reducing image file sizes using complex algorithms. There are two types: lossless, which does not affect the quality of the image; and lossy which sacrifices some quality in favor of smaller files.

Contiguous
This is an option for tools such as the Magic Wand: when enabled only the local area around the cursor will be affected; otherwise instances will be selected from the entire document.

Constrain
Forcing the direction of movement when using a particular tool, usually adhering to 45° angles. This is often used to ensure layers remain aligned when they are moved around the artwork.

Constrain proportions
When enabled this function maintains the dimensions when resizing an image, shape or bounding box. When used with the marquee tools it ensures a perfectly circular or square selection.

Cropping
Reducing the frame around an image to focus on an area of interest.

Depth of field

This is the area of the image that remains in sharp focus whilst the rest is left softer. The technique is often used to draw attention to a point of interest in the picture.

Desaturate

Removing the color information of an image leaving only grayscale tones describing the shadows, midtones and highlights.

Dingbat

A font style that uses monotone images in place of standard letter characters. These can be anything from a simple symbol to a famous person's face. Being text, all the same effects can be applied as you would normally.

Displacement

A method of distorting an image according to the brightness values in an associated grayscale image file.

Distribute

A method of arranging layers to produce equal spacing between their centers or edges.

Dithering

The method of making an image appear to have more colors than it actually has by creating a patterned transition with a mixture of the available colors.

Dots per inch (DPI)

A measure of the output resolution of an image. On-screen images are typically displayed at 72 or 96 dpi whilst professional quality prints are 300dpi or sometimes more.

Feathering

The method of smoothing and blending a selection to avoid jagged edges. This differs from anti-aliasing as the edge is blurred against the destination rather than bridging using a gradient.

Filter gallery

The dialog that lets you browse and apply individual filters or stack several filters together as layers to achieve different effects. These can be previewed prior to committing them to the image.

Gaussian blur

A filter that uses a bell-shaped curve to give the impression of soft focus.

Gaussian noise

A filter that adds random pixels in black and white (or in color) to create the effect of tight texture.

GIF

A lossy file format used in the early days of the internet. Today, GIF images are used for creating animations, a feature not possible with most other file formats.

Graphics tablet

A device connected to the computer that allows you to control the cursor with a pen-shaped stylus instead of a mouse. Many are pressure-sensitive allowing much more accurate control of the tools.

Grayscale

An image composed of black, white and shades of gray, with no color component.

Hard Light

A blend mode in which midtone gray is invisible, leaving just the highlights and shadows on view.

Hue/saturation

An adjustment method used for changing the color of layers and images.

Interpolation

This is the method of resizing up or down by adding or removing pixels. When upsizing an algorithm works out the average between adjacent pixels and places new ones in between.

JPEG

A method of compressing images to take up less space on disk. JPEG files can have a variety of settings, offering smaller file sizes at the expense of some quality.

Layer

All images in Elements consist of at least one layer: they are equivalent to laying sheets of acetate on top of each other to build up areas of the artwork.

Layer linking

Layers can be linked together allowing them to be moved and transformed as a single item. This is useful if you need to uniformly reposition or scale multiple sections of the artwork

Layer mask

Masks are used to selectively hide parts of the artwork by painting in shades of gray: black hides the area, white reveals it, and anything in between makes it transparent.

Glossary

Layer style

These add effects to a layer without permanently affecting the artwork. Examples include: drop shadows, bevels and glows. These can be combined and their attributes adjusted to suit the image.

Leading

The adjustable spacing between lines of text. The term originates from the early days of printing where lead blocks were placed to keep the type separated.

Levels

An adjustment dialog for correcting and enhancing the shadows, midtones and highlights of a photo. They can be applied to the image as a whole or to the individual color channels for finer control.

Liquify

A powerful self-contained filter with which you can distort an image as though it were oil floating on water. This is very useful for flowing, organic substances and also for retouching photos.

Magic Wand

A selection tool that finds areas of the image of a similar color to the area in which the tool is clicked. Commonly used for selecting and removing backgrounds.

Marquee

This is the outline that defines a selection. It's often called the 'marching ants' because of its continuously moving dotted line.

Merge

The Merge Down command will combine one layer with the layer directly beneath it. Merge Visible will produce a single layer from all visible layers in the artwork.

Modifier keys

The keys ctrl, shift and alt that provide additional functions when held down in conjunction with certain tools, usually serving as shortcuts for switching between the tool's modes.

Non-destructive

A term used to describe an effect which does not permanently alter the image and remains editable, even after the image is saved and reopened.

Opacity

Determines how transparent the content of a layer appears. 0% is completely invisible, 100% is solid. Adjusting this value can be used for blending components of the artwork or for creating special effects.

Options bar

The contextual toolbar that sits across the top of the Elements window. This provides specific options and controls for the currently selected tool.

Out-of-bounds

A framing technique where parts of the image extend outside of the frame's boundaries: often used to emphasize the action of a photo.

Painting tools

Any tool such as the Brush, Clone tool, Smudge tool and so on, that affects the area of an image over which it is dragged.

Palette

An area in the workspace containing sets of items such as styles, brushes or layers. These can be collapsed or hidden away when not in use.

Preset manager

A dialog with which you can load, save and organize any brushes, gradients, color swatches and patterns you may have downloaded or created, along with the program's built-in presets.

Photoshop CS3

The 'big brother' of Elements, which offers superior controls and a range of additional features.

Pixel

A loose abbreviation of Picture Element: the individual dots which make up a digital image; each can be one of the millions of colors available.

Pixellation

Visible degradation often caused by scaling the image larger than its original size. This is also used to describe the stepping effect when ant-aliasing is disabled.

Print size

A viewing mode in which an image is displayed at approximately the size it will print, using the current resolution settings.

RAM

Random Access Memory: the part of the computer that holds running programs and their data; for Elements this would be open images and the undo history.

Raster image

An image that is formed of individually colored dots (pixels). This is the most commonly used format for digital painting and photo editing.

Resolution

The method of describing the quality of a digital image by the number of individual pixels it contains. The higher the resolution, the more defined the areas of the picture can be.

RGB

Abbreviation for Red, Green, Blue – the colors used by a computer monitor for displaying images.

Saturation

The depth and intensity of the colors in an image.

Scratch disk

A special area of the computer's hard drive reserved for temporary data storage when system RAM is running low.

Scrubby slider

An alternative method of increasing and decreasing the value of a particular attribute in some dialogs by positioning the cursor over the value and dragging right or left.

Shadows/highlights

An adjustment method for recovering image data from the darkest and brightest parts of an image, without affecting the midtones.

Simplify

Also referred to as rasterizing. The method of converting a shape or text layer to a regular bitmap layer; this can also be applied to layer styles to make them permanent.

Smart Fix

A simple method of automatically enhancing images that requires minimal technical knowledge on the part of the user.

sRGB

A color space devised to make graphic elements look better on computer screens. sRGB is a limited space that's best avoided for printing purposes.

Swatches

A collection of favorite colors and gradients stored in an easily selectable palette.

TIFF

A lossless image file format (see JPEG). Some digital cameras have the option of saving images in TIFF format.

Tolerance

This setting determines the precision of the associated tool. The higher the value, the larger the area of similar tones will be affected and vice versa.

Unsharp mask

An adjustment that attempts to make the image appear crisper by enhancing the contrasting edges. The 'mask' element allows the area of the effect to be fine-tuned by means of a tolerance-like setting.

Vanishing point

Used when working or drawing in perspective: these mark the position on the horizon where two or more lines converge such as looking down a straight road or railway tracks.

Vector graphics

A way of creating images using interconnected points, lines and curves generated by mathematical formulae. Unlike pixel based artwork they can be scaled to any size without losing definition.

Visibility (layer styles)

Similar to changing a layer's Opacity except it only affects the pixels of the layer, leaving the style itself untouched. The three modes, Show, Hide and Ghosted, turn the pixels on and off or render them semi-transparent.

Project files

This symbol indicates that you'll find an Elements file on the CD to accompany the tutorial. They're in a folder called Tutorial Files, and each one includes the starting point for each workthrough. Project files are sorted according to the chapter to which they belong, and each file has a name that relates to the headline on that page.

This symbol means that there's also a QuickTime movie on the CD that shows the tutorial played out in real time. Sometimes it's easier to understand a concept when you see it acted out live, rather than just by reading about it. They're in the Quicktime Movies folder. To view them, you'll need the free QuickTime player from www.apple.com/quicktime, if you don't already have it installed.

Layer mask file

Unlike Photoshop, Elements doesn't support Layer Masks. Well, yes it does – but it can't create them. Elements can, however, import a file containing Layer Masks that was created in Photoshop and then make full use of it. You'll find full instructions on how to use this file on page 42.

Shapes

The custom Jigsaw pattern shapes, as described on page 224. We've also included a small selection of stars so you can make your own starbursts to place behind text announcements.

To use them, open the Goodies folder on the CD and copy the file **Cheat.csh** to the folder C:*Program Files\Adobe Photoshop Elements 6.0\Presets* on your hard drive.

When you restart Elements, the styles will show up in the Cheat section of the Shapes menu.

Star 30 big   Star 20 big

Star 20 small   Star 30 small

Above:
Jigsaw
Landscape

Left:
Jigsaw
Portrait

Layer styles

Elements 6 has lost the Inner Shadow style found in previous versions – so we've made some for you, along with a selection of neon and metallic text effect styles.

To use these styles, open the Goodies folder on the CD. Copy the file **Cheat.asl** to the folder C:*Documents and Settings\All Users\Application Data\Adobe\ Photoshop Elements\6.0\Locale\en_US\Photo Creations\ layer styles* on your hard drive. Then put the file **Cheat. xml** into the folder C:*Documents and Settings\All Users\Application Data\Adobe\Photoshop Elements\6.0\ Locale\en_US\Photo Creations Metadata\Layer Styles.* (The folder en_US should be the locality folder for your country of residence.)

When you restart Elements, the styles will show up as Cheat Styles in the Styles menu.

Inner shadow big soft

Inner shadow big softer

Inner shadow small soft

Inner shadow small

Inner shadow big hard

Inner shadow edge

Neon blue

Neon blue 2

Neon pink

Neon green

Neon red

Neon yellow

Metal bling

Metal chunky gold

Metal chunky chrome

Metal rust

Metal chunky gold 2

Metal chunky chrome 2

245

Index